Praise for

SELF-MADE BOSS

A small business doesn't come with an owner's manual . . . until now. Drawing on their extensive experience working with small business owners, Jackie Reses and Lauren Weinberg share the stories and tips you need to help your business thrive.

> —**Adam Grant,** #1 *New York Times* bestselling author of
> *Think Again* and host of the TED podcast *WorkLife*

We started Shake Shack as a humble hot dog cart to raise money for a public park in NYC and never dreamed it would become a global public company. I've lived so many of the challenges that small business owners experience and this read provides the nuts-and-bolts guide every entrepreneur can get their arms around.

> —**Randy Garruti,** CEO, Shake Shack

Small business is part of our ethos at M&T Bank. Helping entrepreneurs grow their businesses—and themselves—through mentorship and resources is some of our most important work. We all need a community of advisors to instruct and inspire us, and that's what Jackie and Lauren have created in this book for business owners everywhere.

> —**Rene F. Jones,** chairman and CEO, M&T Bank

When small businesses thrive, so does the entire economy. *Self-Made Boss* is teeming with actionable insights to help small businesses succeed, no matter the obstacles ahead.

> —**Karen G. Mills,** Harvard Business School Senior Fellow,
> former SBA administrator and Obama cabinet member

As always, Jackie and Lauren have provided us with sound advice. Use this book as your go-to manual with practical and real information. I loved reading the stories about the amazing small business owners who started with nothing and were able to make it happen.

> —**Gregg Renfrew,** CEO Beautycounter

Learning from mentors and a community of other business builders is key to my success as a serial entrepreneur. Jackie and Lauren have been mentors to thousands of small businesses, and their work helped millions more. *Self-Made Boss* is an impressive distillation of wisdom from years in the trenches, and I love how they tie highly relevant stories to insightful lessons.

> —**Joe Lonsdale,** cofounder of Palantir, Addepar, Resilience Bio, and Partner, 8VC

Many of us dream of starting our own business. But how do we make those dreams a reality? Entrepreneur and small business gurus Reses and Weinberg share the real deal on what really matters when starting—and growing—a sustainable business. Their lessons from thousands of small business owners won't just save you time and money, they will help you love what you do that much more.

> —**Lisa Kay Solomon,** coauthor of the bestselling books *Moments of Impact* and *Design a Better Business*

Jackie ties together her formative experiences, applies her Wharton-honed insights, and extends the leadership I have seen firsthand in her service as an alumna to others through this book. Readers will benefit from the book's wit, wisdom, and empathy, and the depths of her interest in businesses of all types in varying sectors. She embodies the entrepreneurial spirit we strive to inspire at Wharton.

> —**Erika H. James,** Dean and Reliance Professor of Management and Private Enterprise, The Wharton School

There are great entrepreneurs and there are thoughtful students of business. Jackie and Lauren are both, and it makes this book an important one. The US economy is much more likely to succeed if entrepreneurs succeed. And entrepreneurs are much more likely to succeed if they heed this important book's wisdom.

> —**Laurence H. Summers,** a Charles W. Eliot University Professor and President Emeritus at Harvard University, the 71st Secretary of the Treasury under President Clinton, and director of the National Economic Council under President Obama

Jackie and Lauren have worked with thousands of small business owners across multiple companies. They have distilled so many crucial lessons, resources, and tools here that the book is literally a how-to guide to helping your company succeed. And the learnings are well delivered—accessible, engaging, and practical.

> —**Allan Thygesen,** President Americas & Global Partners, Google

SELF-MADE
BOSS

ADVICE, HACKS, AND LESSONS
FROM SMALL BUSINESS OWNERS

JACKIE RESES

LAUREN WEINBERG

McGraw Hill

New York Chicago San Francisco Athens London Madrid
Mexico City Milan New Delhi Singapore Sydney Toronto

Copyright © 2022 by Jackie Reses and Lauren Weinberg. All rights reserved. Printed in the United States of America. Except as permitted under the United States Copyright Act of 1976, no part of this publication may be reproduced or distributed in any form or by any means, or stored in a database or retrieval system, without the prior written permission of the publisher.

1 2 3 4 5 6 7 8 9   LCR   27 26 25 24 23 22

ISBN   978-1-264-26409-4
MHID   1-264-26409-7

e-ISBN   978-1-264-26410-0
e-MHID   1-264-26410-0

This publication is designed to provide accurate and authoritative information in regard to the subject matter covered. It is sold with the understanding that neither the author nor the publisher is engaged in rendering legal, accounting, securities trading, or other professional services. If legal advice or other expert assistance is required, the services of a competent professional person should be sought.
—*From a Declaration of Principles Jointly Adopted by a Committee of the American Bar Association and a Committee of Publishers and Associations*

Library of Congress Cataloging-in-Publication Data

Names: Reses, Jackie, author. | Weinberg, Lauren (Chief marketing officer), author.
Title: Self-made boss : advice, hacks, and lessons from small business owners / Jackie Reses and Lauren Weinberg.
Description: New York : McGraw Hill, [2022] | Includes bibliographical references and index.
Identifiers: LCCN 2021049892 | ISBN 9781264264094 (hardback) | ISBN 9781264264100 (ebook)
Subjects: LCSH: Small business—Growth. | Entrepreneurship.
Classification: LCC HD62.7 .R4678 2022 | DDC 658.02/2—dc23/eng/20211014
LC record available at https://lccn.loc.gov/2021049892

McGraw Hill books are available at special quantity discounts to use as premiums and sales promotions or for use in corporate training programs. To contact a representative, please visit the Contact Us pages at www.mhprofessional.com.

McGraw Hill is committed to making our products accessible to all learners. To learn more about the available support and accommodations we offer, please contact us at accessibility@mheducation.com. We also participate in the Access Text Network (www.accesstext.org), and ATN members may submit requests through ATN.

*To all of the entrepreneurs and
business owners whose passion,
resilience, fortitude and creativity
inspire us every day.*

Contents

Acknowledgments

Jackie: Forever thankful to my beloved family: Matt, Emilia, Charlotte, and Owen. They make me laugh and think every day. I love you and I'd be lost without you. My parents also showed me how the care of a local business person made a difference in a community. I spent my childhood working at Reses Pharmacy in Pomona, New Jersey, and some of my earliest memories are behind the counter helping to manage the greeting card inventory in a small shop. Life lessons from the pharmacy sit with me every day. I am also thankful to my coauthor and friend, Lauren. This has been a labor of love, and I couldn't think of another person that I would want working on this with me.

Lauren: Thank you to my incredibly supportive family. Jeremy, Ethan, and Ben, you put up with my crazy schedule and have always been my biggest fans. I would never be able to write this book or lean in to my career without your unwavering support. My parents both worked in and owned small businesses. (Fun fact: my dad is featured in this book.) I appreciate the work ethic they instilled in me from a young age. I'd also like to thank Jackie, my partner on this initiative. Jackie has been my mentor and my biggest cheerleader for many years. I am so grateful for Jackie and my other mentors, including Lisa Licht, Kathy Savitt, Mollie Spillman and Nada Stirratt. I've been standing on the shoulders of these incredible women and make an effort to pay it forward every day.

We were lucky to have a lot of help with this book at every stage.

When we were first thinking about the idea, there were many at Square, where both of us worked, who dedicated their personal time to review and support ideas for the book. They include Ed Lin, Eitan Bencuya, Katie Dally, Mallory Russell, Justin Lomax, Zack Ashley and Kelsy Reitz. They were willing to lean in when this was just an idea and a book proposal.

Then, when we moved into finding sellers from across the globe, we enlisted the help of Nelson Murray, Jeff Suppes, Mallory Russell, and Evan Groll. They had an eye for small businesses that had incredible stories to tell and helped us brainstorm titles for the book as well. Mallory, in particular, helped us fine-tune the chapters and areas we would focus on to ensure we hit the most important topics for business owners.

We also needed advice on broadening our network. Samantha Ku, Andy Montgomery, and Audrey Kim went out of their way to support our research with additional insight and ideas. Audrey helped us think about which experts would be helpful to include so that we could get the frameworks organized. Andy gave us feedback on our design and had a critical eye toward the cover.

Andrew Gerlach from Sullivan and Cromwell, Gary Horowitz of Simpson Thatcher, and Ryan LaForce of

Goodwin Procter also provided us first-rate legal insight. Alana White from Giant Spoon provided additional insight about how business owners should think about leveraging traditional media channels for marketing.

Michelle Garcia-Vasquez has been with us the entire time, organizing calls, keeping our drafts in order, managing the process with sellers and experts. She put her heart and soul into our book and took on a huge amount of work to help get this over the finish line! Kate Kapoor took on the final management of our drafts, bios, and photos and dug in with her fantastic organizational skills.

Ingrid Case is our voice. She understood how to jump in and help us bring the stories of our sellers to life. She worked with us throughout the entire process and made us laugh and cry. She interviewed every small business included in this book and brought the stories to life. Tyler Lechtenberg helped us on projects while we were at Square and once again helped in crafting these stories. He and his colleagues at Fenway Strategies, such as Sam Koppelman, live in rarified writing air . . . and we are thankful for their advice, edits, and voice.

Jack Dorsey didn't write one word of this book. He did inspire us with his steadfast focus on how important the small business economy is, and how we need to create tools to help them thrive. His passion is inspiring and will always be a part of the story of how this book came to be.

Most of all, we want to thank all of the entrepreneurs, business owners, and experts who shared their stories and advice so freely. We're proud to know you.

Prologue

A Letter to Our Readers

Jackie: For four years, I traveled across the United States, a country with more food trucks and beauty salons, coffee bars, and record shops than anyone could possibly visit in one life span—let alone four years. That didn't stop me from trying, though.

At the time, getting to know our country's small businesses was a big part of my job. I ran the small business lending and banking business at Square. I believed deeply not just in crunching numbers and optimizing machine learning credit algorithms, but in actually talking to small business owners to truly understand their goals and challenges, sample their goods, and listen to their stories. I was part business advisor, part solutions creator, part psychiatrist.

And for four years, all across the country, I spent a lot of my time applying those skills. From Philadelphia to Minnetonka, Atlanta to Santa Rosa, I crisscrossed the country to meet these extraordinary entrepreneurs and hear their stories.

I met Kelly Kondah, who'd owned Colossal Cupcakes in Ohio, and talked about her approach to decor in her retail stores. I spent time with Courtney Foster, a one-chair beauty salon owner in New York City. I bought flowers from Jen Pratt, whose flower truck in Idaho brightens an entire community's birthdays and Mother's Days. I ate turkey legs with Philip Webber at his food truck in North Carolina. I even sampled the beats of Andrew Hypes, a DJ in Virginia.

Nearly everyone I spoke with—whether they'd invented a new snack for kids or operated a brick-and-mortar restaurant that had been passed down from their parents, whether they were running a bubble tea chain or a plastic surgery business—had something insightful to share about what it took to build, run, and grow a company.

Maybe it was a 60-year-old boosting sales by becoming a social media savant. Maybe it was an oyster farmer reinventing his business in the middle of a global pandemic. Maybe it was an entrepreneur who refused to be defined, or denied, because of her race and gender.

No matter the details, I was amazed by the wisdom and insights that each business owner could offer. They knew their stuff. The more I heard from them, the more I wanted *other* small business owners to hear from them, too.

Each of these conversations uncovered something else for me: When it comes to getting practical business advice, small business owners are woefully underserved. Sure, you can find all sorts of slick tips from towering CEOs of Fortune 500 companies. But what if you own a restaurant, and you're trying to figure out how to source good fish, or if you own a plumbing supply store and you're trying to crack $1 million in revenue for the first time? You'll be running a lot of Google searches before you hear from someone who's actually stood in your shoes.

I wanted to change that. I became focused on helping these small business owners share their advice—because the story of our country's small businesses is anything but small.

Here in the United States, we have close to 30 million small businesses, and internationally there is comparable depth. I've always known how important they are to our country and the communities that make us who we are, because my parents owned one.

I learned from a young age that when you run the neighborhood pharmacy, as my parents did, there is no such thing as Christmas holiday. When customers were out of important medication on a holiday, they knew to call my family. If they needed a house visit, my parents would come right over. My mom embodied the idea that "the customer is always right" as she stood behind the counter of the pharmacy dealing with people who sometimes wore their stress in their language. It was a priceless learning experience to see business and community wrapped up with the entrepreneurial spirit of a family business.

There are business owners like my parents all across the country, whose employees make up more than half our working economy. But here's the thing: those numbers still don't come close to tallying up what these businesses mean, not just for the people running them, but also for the people who love them. Think about the neighborhood pizza joint your kid's Little League team heads to after a big win or the family-owned hardware store that sold you the part that finally stopped that leaky faucet. Profits alone don't convey the full story of these businesses.

They don't just contribute to our economies. They're part of the fabric that holds our neighborhoods and towns together.

I hope this book reflects that larger story. In these pages, you'll read not just about who these small business owners are, but how they built their companies, step by step. How did they get their start? When did they decide to hire more staff? How did they set a course for growth? And when problems arose, how did they fight through them?

From the example of the dozens of business owners we spoke with for this book, I hope you will take away practical advice and lessons you can put to work right away as you become your own Self-Made Boss.

When I decided to write this book, I spent a lot of time thinking about whose stories I would include in it—but I didn't spend any time contemplating who I needed by my side to write it. From the very beginning, I knew I needed someone who'd lived a lot of these experiences on her own, someone who has seen the ups and downs of owning a small business from many angles. So for me, there was only one person I wanted to be my partner: my brilliant colleague and friend, Lauren Weinberg.

Lauren: Before I became chief marketing officer at Square, I'd been in the corporate world for nearly half my life. I'd led large teams for a major reality television network. I'd served on corporate boards—sometimes with other women, mostly without. I'd had workplaces I loved and jobs where I couldn't wait to clock out. But one experience taught me more than any other: being my own boss.

In the middle of my career, I set out on my own as a consultant, helping both startups and established brands navigate marketing strategy. When I first started my own shop, I thought making the website would be the biggest hurdle. After all, I'd been doing marketing work for decades. I figured I had all the skills I needed—and a Rolodex full of contacts. What else was there to learn?

The answer, as it turned out, was a lot. You know the stuff that *just happens* when you work at someone else's company? When you're running your own company, you have to do all that stuff by yourself. All of it. Applying for an employer identification number. Setting up an LLC. Opening a business bank account. Sending out invoices— and making sure you actually get paid.

For me, that meant that instead of doing what I started my business to do, I was spending an inordinate amount of time plugging numbers into spreadsheets or driving to the bank. The first couple of months were especially rough. Working on my first two or three projects, I made the mistake of telling clients to pay me *after* I finished their project. These projects could go on for months, and during that time, I didn't get paid.

I found out quickly just how steep the learning curve was going to be. During my time at Square, I saw that this constant learning and balancing act was all too familiar to so many of our sellers.

Since 2017, like Jackie, I've been listening to small businesses of every shape and size, helping them tell their stories and grow their companies. During conversations, in research data and survey responses, at educational events for sellers, and in the lead-up to big marketing launches, I kept hearing the same thing: One of the biggest struggles for any small business is feeling like you're stretched too thin. If you run a food truck, you're not only the chef, you're also the accountant. In a bookstore, you're not just in charge of choosing the latest titles and booking local authors for readings, you're also responsible for building a social media presence. It's part of what makes being a small business owner such a shot of adrenaline. But it doesn't make things any easier.

When the Covid-19 pandemic hit in 2020, a big part of my job became reaching out to these entrepreneurs, hearing about how they were weathering a storm for which no one had time to prepare. When cities were locked down and in-person sales plummeted, small business owners were forced to adapt or close their doors, maybe forever. The stories I heard of business owners who shifted their focus, who retooled their business plans, who scraped and clawed just to stay afloat—those stories once again proved to me the brilliance and resilience that defines this community of small business owners.

Not every year will bring a pandemic, of course. But every year—every day—will bring its own new challenges. That's why Jackie and I wrote this book. We hope it can help you avoid common pitfalls, or at least help you navigate through some of these roadblocks. We hope that you can spend less time worrying about the things you're not an expert in—like running HR or setting up a profit-and-loss statement—and more time doing what you love. And we hope, more than anything, that you won't feel alone, because you'll know that even if you run your business by yourself, you are part of a community of small business owners who keep our economy, and our country, running.

Now, we know how busy you are, so we designed this book to be easy to read. Before you get started, here are a few tips about how you can use it:

- **You don't have to read it cover to cover.** Think about it as a reference guide, something you can flip to when you come across a new challenge. If you want to read about managing your finances, go to Chapter 5. If you want to learn more about marketing, head to Chapter 6. We hope to provide you with some answers—or at least, a good starting place.

- **We've got something for you, no matter the stage of your business.** If you're just starting out, you might want to check out our introductory chapters on starting a business (Chapter 1), creating a business plan (Chapter 2), and operations and logistics (Chapter 4). If you've been doing this a while and are feeling stuck, you might find inspiration in our chapters on roadblocks (Chapter 8) or growth and scale (Chapter 9).

- **This is a starter kit.** We try to identify and cover just about any problem you might come across and give you the hard-earned wisdom of other small business owners like you. We recognize that sometimes, you might need to go further to get really in the weeds on a given topic—like your tax strategy or structuring an acquisition. That's when you'll want to find another resource or even hire experts who can help you with your specific questions. Throughout the book, we've made sure to provide advice on where to turn if you need further answers.

- **It's a chance to spur reflection—and generate plans.**
  At the end of each chapter, we've included questions that you may want to consider. It's worth thinking ahead and gaming out possible scenarios. Even if a decision doesn't feel especially pressing right now, it almost certainly will someday.

As you'll read in these pages, there's no specific road map for any small business owner. That's the beauty—and the risk—of being your own boss. But no matter how you decided to start your business, or where you're thinking about taking it, there's a common purpose that all small business owners share. In fact, it's more than a purpose. It's an identity, one defined not by what you do but by who you are.

It's the drive to build something from the ground up. It's the relentless pursuit of turning obstacles into opportunities, roadblocks into stepping-stones. It's the commitment to throwing everything you've got into your business, being willing to spend hours ordering inventory and balancing your sheets, putting every spare dollar back into your dream. It's tough and messy, hard-fought and hard-won. And above all, it's something you can't have when you work anywhere else—or for anyone else.

That's what it means to be a Self-Made Boss.

Welcome to the club.

SELF-MADE
BOSS

CHAPTER 1

Taking the First Step

Two months into her job at a biotech startup, Meenal Lele read an article in a medical journal that changed the course of her life. For the first time, researchers had found that exposing children to small amounts of common allergens early in their lives could prevent them from developing allergies. For Meenal, reading this was a mixed blessing.

On the one hand, this news made her "kind of furious," because her 11-month-old child had already developed severe allergies to eggs, peanuts, and tree nuts—in other words, it was too late to help him avoid allergies. But on the other hand, she finally had steps she could take that might help her other children remain allergy-free. So she started preparing microscopic amounts of foods like eggs and peanuts for him to try.

As it turned out, doing this in a way that was safe for many babies to eat—while making sure she didn't

1

Meenal Lele

Meenal Lele is founder and CEO of Lil Mixins, an allergy prevention company. She previously led the clinical studies and education that brought the Subchondroplasty procedure (acquired by Zimmer) and PIVO blood collection (acquired by BD) to market. She has an engineering and a business degree from the University of Pennsylvania.

contaminate her kitchen and endanger her older child—was easier said than done, even for someone who had spent her career pioneering innovations in biotech. She remembers asking herself endless questions: "How finely ground is fine enough? How many grams of protein are in a peanut?"

There had to be a better way, Meenal concluded, but she couldn't find it anywhere. So she decided to create her own solution. After two and a half years of experimentation, she pulled it off, creating Lil Mixins, a company that sells supplements with precisely measured amounts of common allergens to help children build a tolerance to them before it's too late.

It's a smart business that improves people's lives—and it all came from Meenal's life experience.

◆　◆　◆

Based in Philadelphia, Pennsylvania, Lil Mixins is just one of those 30 million American small businesses we told you about in our Prologue. Each one has its own origin story.

Many entrepreneurs start their companies for the same reason Meenal did: they see a problem in the world and decide to become part of the solution. Of course, there are other reasons to start a small business too, whether you have an itch to strike out on your own, build on a family legacy, turn a passion into a profession, or give back to your community. Throughout this book, you'll hear from entrepreneurs who took the leap of faith to start a company for all these reasons. In every instance, they had an idea they were excited about and a plan to bring it to life.

In this chapter, we're focusing on that initial spark, the idea that spurs you to start your business in the first place. Because along the way, running your business will only get harder—trust us. If you can remember why you began the work in the first place, it will help keep the tough days in perspective.

Being Your Own Boss

Drafted out of college, Bobby Crocker played Major League Baseball as an outfielder for the Oakland Athletics. When a shoulder injury ended his baseball career, he knew he needed another way to make a living.

Bobby Crocker
Bobby Crocker owns LVLUP Fitness, a personalized training service in California's Bay Area. He is an ex-professional baseball player.

"I did interviews with other companies, but I kept landing back on wanting my independence," Bobby says. "I remember watching my dad run a construction business. Like him, I feel a big motivation to be able to provide for myself and my family on my own terms. It gave me a sense of pride and purpose."

Six years ago, Bobby began working as a self-employed personal trainer in the Bay Area, helping his clients build their fitness and their confidence. He loves the independence, he says, though he found aspects of it challenging at first.

"In baseball, the framework was provided for me," Bobby says. "I knew what I would do every day, and I felt responsible for executing that schedule. Creating a framework for myself took some time." In this way, for Bobby, being able to create his schedule, strategy, and relationships had positives and negatives: what he gained in freedom he lost in structure.

Carrying on the Family Business

Aylon Pesso
Together with his father, Aylon Pesso owns and runs Pesso's Ices & Ice Cream in Bayside, New York. His favorite ice cream flavor is roasted marshmallow.

Bobby is a solo act, but plenty of entrepreneurs become involved in small businesses alongside their family members. Aylon Pesso, for instance, co-owns an ice cream shop, Pesso's Ices & Ice Cream, in Queens, New York, with his father.

The family has been in the dessert business since Aylon's early adolescence when his father, Gidon Pesso, a serial entrepreneur then working as a house painter, decided to try his hand at ice cream.

Aylon scooped ice cream through high school and took over the store's social media, website, and marketing in college. After graduating, he went back to work with his father, eventually becoming part owner and vice president of operations.

Aylon has an older brother, but he wasn't interested in the family business. "I was closer to our dad, maybe more like-thinking," he says. "That's helped us make it work. We can look at something, give each other a look, and know what we have to do to make it work."

For a long time, Aylon recalls, they offered 132 flavors every day, all made on-site in small batches. Now they use data from their point-of-sale system to understand which of their 60 flavors are making money.

"The ice-cream trade is a good business," he says. "Ice cream gives people joy, and they get to give that experience to other people. I make something with my hands that will make someone happy."

And even though working with family can bring challenges—as we'll discuss in later chapters—when you are able to put smiles on the faces of customers alongside your loved ones, it can be that much sweeter.

Pursuing a Personal Passion

The enthusiasm Aylon Pesso feels for ice cream, Peter Stein feels for oysters. "I can't remember a day that I didn't love oysters," he says. "On a calorie basis, oysters are the most sustainable and nutritious food source in the world. They're high in all the good things and low in all the bad things."

Peter Stein

Peter Stein owns Peeko Oysters, which is on Long Island near New Suffolk, NY. He can't remember a time when he didn't love oysters.

Peter had been a business management consultant, a New York classroom teacher, and an education software employee. Then he was laid off, and he did some soul-searching.

"I grew up coming to the East End of Long Island on the weekends and in the summer," he said. "I loved fishing with my dad, and my dad loved oysters as well. When I had a blank spot in my career, I went back to what I had always loved."

That's when he set out to build Peeko Oysters in Little Peconic Bay on Long Island. As you'll read in Chapters 4 and 8, he's become quite a success. Today, restaurants all over the New York area sell his Peeko oysters to their customers, and the retail side of the business is thriving too. Peter's lifelong passion is still going strong.

Making a Living After a Life Transition

Like Peter, many business owners start companies in response to a personal transition: being laid off, returning to work after spending years as a full-time parent, or pivoting to a new industry after retirement.

Jen Pratt, for instance, started Fresh Sunshine Flowers in Sandpoint, Idaho, after her employer, clothing company Coldwater Creek, closed its doors in 2014. "My mom was a florist, and I grew up helping and learning from her," Jen says. But building a brick-and-mortar floral business from the ground up was a daunting prospect. It meant high overhead costs, like rent or a mortgage, not to mention utilities. So Jen started her florist operation in a white box truck with a side window.

Jen Pratt

Jen Pratt owns Fresh Sunshine Flowers in Sandpoint, ID. She began her business by selling out of a box truck with a side window, back when food trucks were at their peak.

Jen bought her truck in May. A graphic designer friend helped Jen come up with a logo, and another friend helped design decals to put on the truck. A third buddy helped her gut and build out the truck, and a fourth friend, this one a mechanic, got the truck in running order. By July 4, Jen was ready to roll out her floral spin on a food truck, offering up bouquets that were red, white, blue, and every color in between.

Giving Back to Your Community

Erin Caudell and her partner, Franklin Pleasant, believe that everyone should have access to safe, nutritious food. Through The Local Grocer, based in Flint, Michigan, they are putting that belief into practice.

Before they could do that, though, Erin and Franklin needed to get a farm—so they took out a loan and bought 10 acres from a county land bank that holds foreclosed properties. They started growing dozens of different kinds of organic vegetables.

Erin Caudell

Erin Caudell and her partner, Franklin Pleasant, co-own The Local Grocer in Flint, MI. They are longtime food activists and newer farmers, working to make sure every community has access to nutrient-dense foods.

The Local Grocer has also teamed up with two other local farms as part of a community-supported agriculture (CSA) program, which allows families in the region to sign up for regular deliveries of a wide range of crops, from sweet corn and winter squash to broccoli and cauliflower.

They also participate in farmers markets, run a catering business, rent out their commercial kitchen, and sell their own and other farmers' products directly to buyers. "We've probably worked with 25 different farmers to buy for the store," Erin says. "We see this as a business incubator where we can give feedback and learn something ourselves.

"Franklin and I take part-time jobs here and there, especially in the winter, to make this work," she says. The hope is that The Local Grocer will eventually support the couple and their two children.

Filling a Gap: Build the Business You Want to Patronize

When photographer Lucia Rollow graduated from New York's School of Visual Arts, she couldn't afford access to a darkroom. One day, when she was complaining about this to a neighbor, she learned that her building was renting storage spaces in the basement for $75 a month.

Lucia rented one and set up a darkroom in that space. When she started telling friends about it, she quickly came to realize that she wasn't the only one in Brooklyn who needed a place to develop film. It wasn't long before her little idea had a big following of paying customers.

A year later, Lucia had earned enough to move her business, which she called the Brooklyn Community Darkroom, into a storefront. In 2015, the darkroom moved to its current location in the Bushwick neighborhood. Now called the Bushwick Community Darkroom, it rents out darkroom time and offers development services and classes in developing and printing to an audience that ranges from beginners to professional photographers. "The goal is to support a community of photographers," Lucia says. "Someone with any level of knowledge or experience can come and learn." About 500 photographers use the facility every month.

Lucia runs the darkroom with a staff of 10 part-time employees, each working between one and three days a week. She relishes being in charge. "Now that I've had this flexibility," she says, "I don't think I could handle the lack of flexibility of working for someone else."

Lucia Rollow

Lucia Rollow owns Bushwick Community Darkroom in Brooklyn, NY. A graduate of New York's School of Visual Arts, Rollow's first darkroom was a storage cubby in the basement of her apartment building.

Same Picture, Different Details

No matter what kind of business they're in, or why they started it, all small business owners have a common struggle. They're all working to figure out how to best take an idea and turn it into a reality—and make a living while they're at it.

Small businesses might look very different from the outside, but in reality, most are quite similar. Aylon Pesso sells ice cream and Jen Pratt sells flowers, but they both need to set up their finances and legally incorporate. They both hire help, run business operations, build their brands, decide how to grow and scale, and have to get past roadblocks. And they both may eventually transition away from the business they've built and step into whatever comes next.

If you're starting or running a small business, you'll have to do those things, too. You probably don't sell oysters or make dietary supplements out of common allergens. But at root, your challenges and concerns will probably look a lot like the ones that Peter and Meenal face.

That's why we wrote this book. We learned a lot hearing about how each of these business owners built their business. And we believe that you will, too.

Find and Use Free Resources

Before we dive into more of these Self-Made Bosses' stories, we'd be remiss if we didn't point out the free public resources that can help you start and grow your small business. The Small Business Administration (SBA), for instance, is a federal agency that gives out a treasure trove of free resources.

"The SBA is the best-kept secret in the federal government," says Bill Briggs, who worked for the SBA for three and a half years. "Going there is like going to a library for a small business that has very helpful librarians. They've seen your problems before and can help you do the right things and avoid the pitfalls."

The SBA and its resource centers can help you:

SPECIALIST

Bill Briggs
Bill Briggs is former acting associate administrator, Office of Capital Access, a division of the Small Business Administration. Currently he works as a consultant in Arlington, VA. Running the 2020 Paycheck Protection Program is his proudest professional achievement.

- Explore a new idea
- Write a business plan
- Find a mentor or coach
- Grow your business
- Get a loan
- Find grants
- Put your personal and business finances in order
- Start or improve any part of your business
- Draw up initial contracts

"The biggest mistake entrepreneurs make is not using the SBA network," Bill says. "Google 'SBA resources' in your state. They will help you even if you just have an idea. Have hope and have patience—people out there want to help you."

You can also take advantage of locally based help. Local chambers of commerce may offer valuable resources, including education and access to partners that can help you get started. There are also specialized chambers of commerce that support specific demographic groups, like the Black Chamber of Commerce or the Hispanic Chamber of Commerce.

Many other free resources can also help guide your business formation. To start and run the Bushwick Community Darkroom, for instance, Lucia Rollow used Start Small Think Big (www.startsmallthinkbig.org), a nonprofit that helps under-resourced entrepreneurs create businesses in underserved areas. "If I had used them back in the beginning, starting this business would have been a lot easier," she says.

In fact, Lucia says, New York and many other locations around the United States have free public resources for entrepreneurs. "Start with your city's website," she suggests. "Look for a section on small business resources. Do a Google search. If you're a woman or a member of a minority group, look for services to support you specifically." You might be surprised at what you find in your local community.

More important, enjoy the jump! It's daunting, emotionally challenging, and may very well become your life's work. With those stakes in mind, take the time to think through how you will start, run, and grow your business.

It's the first step to becoming a Self-Made Boss.

Questions to Consider

- Will you like being your own boss? Do you prefer dictating your own schedule—or are you the kind of person who needs more structure?

- What are your passions? Could you turn them into a career?

- What kind of businesses do you *wish* existed? Could you be the person to make one of them happen?

- Do you have a support network of friends and family who can advise you or provide other support?

- Are you okay with uncertainty? Are you the kind of person that is willing to ride out the ups and downs? If so, when are you going to get started?

SELF-MADE
BOSSES

Michael Lassner

Jordan Rosner

Lisa O'Kelly

Jen Pratt

CHAPTER 2

Creating a Business Plan

Michael Lassner is a man with a plan—in fact, he's a man with many plans. That's because, when he started Allied Steel Buildings, he paid the price for not having one.

In the early days, Michael and his business partner ran their company out of an apartment in Fort Lauderdale, Florida. They were so busy doing the work in front of them that they didn't make time to think about what came next.

Over the years, however, it became clear that the pair had different visions for their future. Michael's partner wanted to stay smaller and closer to home, working on simpler projects. Michael wanted to make the business bigger, more global, and more complex.

"The first year was great. A year or two later, we began to wonder if we were right for each other," Michael says.

"Clarity around our business plan was the missing piece. We were looking at how we can be successful today rather than at where we were going. If we'd done that, we would have realized that this wasn't the right partnership."

After buying out his former partner, Michael focused on building alignment with his team so that everyone would be on the same page about their purpose. Today, he and his employees maintain an ongoing business plan.

"We think about our goals and the markets we're in, and we plan around opportunities in particular markets," he says. "We do postmortems, too. Here was the plan, what happened, what can we learn. We always learn something."

Now? Michael says he has "plans within plans—not just a long-term goal of entering a new market, but a plan for how to actually accomplish it," and he thinks all small business owners should do the same—to analyze not only where they are, but where they want to go and how they're going to get there.

In this chapter, we will show you how to do exactly that.

Michael Lassner
Michael Lassner, president of Allied Steel Buildings, is disrupting the global steel construction industry. He believes success is created by modeling business strategies around client needs. Michael leads an international team of innovators, who tirelessly work daily to deliver on the promise of clients first.

The Blueprint for Your Business

Small businesses have about a 50-50 chance of surviving the first five years—and one in five doesn't even make it a full 12 months, according to the US Bureau of Labor Statistics.

Michael was lucky to be able to buy out his partner and run the company his own way. But businesses have a much better shot at long-term survival and success if they lay out their vision for the future before, not after, they start running it.

This means writing a business plan, and it's one of the most important steps in building a successful company. Sometimes this business plan is written for public consumption. For instance, if you would like anyone else to put money into your company—which could be in the form of a grant, stock shares, or a loan—you will need a polished business plan. A bank will certainly want to see one before approving a loan. Your family and friends might have fewer requirements before sending you a check, but a written plan will still help set their minds at ease by demonstrating that you're taking your venture seriously.

Even if you don't intend to take loans or outside investors, and even if you don't have anyone to read your business plan, systematically thinking through a blueprint is still critical. Yvonne Cariveau, director of the Center for Innovation & Entrepreneurship at Minnesota State University's College of Business, is an expert on business plans. She says that you don't necessarily need to write out a buttoned-up essay, but you do need to do the thinking

SPECIALIST

Yvonne Cariveau
Yvonne Cariveau
directs the Center
for Innovation &
Entrepreneurship
at Minnesota
State University in
Mankato, MN. She
teaches classes on
entrepreneurship
and has been an
entrepreneur herself
for 28 years with her
business, Internet
Connections, Inc.

and research that a business plan forces you to perform.

That's what Jordan Rosner did when she opened her photography business in Millburn, New Jersey. She researched her industry, wrote up a plan, put it in a drawer, and hasn't looked at it since. What she learned in the process of writing the plan, however, has stayed with her every day. She says thinking about how she was going to approach every element of her business is what's helped make her business a success.

Like Jordan, you might end up doing the research, writing a rough draft, and stopping there—using your business plan for internal purposes. Or you might draft an externally facing plan: perhaps one for bankers or venture capitalists, one for individual investors, one for potential business partners, and one for yourself. The information in these documents won't change, but the focus will shift toward the things you think a particular audience will want to know.

A business plan has multiple sections, each of which is described briefly in this chapter.

An Executive Summary

A good executive summary pops. It should grab the reader and explain, succinctly and compellingly, why your business will succeed. You'll want to explain briefly what's in the rest of the document, particularly the problem, solution, and audience, so that readers will understand what you're doing and why. Tell your story as vividly as you can. Another tip: Write the summary last. It should be a greatest hits, of sorts, for what's to come. Just because it's short doesn't mean it's not important; it might be the most critical part of the entire document.

Jordan Rosner
Jordan Rosner is a photographer in Millburn, NJ. She got her start in photography in high school and worked for local newspapers after completing a degree in photojournalism from Lehigh University.

The Management Team

Your plan should include bios of the owners and key employees of the business, particularly if they have relevant experience for the new situation. Each person's bio can be as short as a few bullet points or a few paragraphs that highlight what's relevant. You don't need to include every step of your career; be selective and decide how best to present yourself. Explain what qualifies each person for his or her role.

Your team members don't need to have worked in your industry, but you do need to draw parallels between the work they've done and the skills you'll need from your company's management team. If you haven't spent much time in your industry yet, an advisory board of people with relevant experience can help round out your team.

Problem, Solution, and Audience

Most businesses exist to solve a problem, such as selling a product that customers can't get nearby or offering a new or better service than what's already on the market. But before you decide that your solution is *the* solution, spend more time listening to other people talk about the problem.

Do your research, no matter what field you are in. "Define your problem very, very specifically. Observe. Ask open-ended questions," Yvonne says. Cariveau likes to snowshoe, for example, but finds it awkward to attach her snowshoes' back binding to her boots. If she were thinking of making a product to solve that problem, she says, she would go and watch people put on snowshoes. Where do they hit problems? Do the difficulties involve flexibility, cold fingers, stiff plastic, or bindings that are too short? The point is, refine your idea and then refine it some more. Even after you launch your product, listen to customer feedback and keep iterating.

"Entrepreneurs fall in love with their solutions before they really understand the problem," she explains. Is the problem you're considering actually worth solving? Is the solution worth tons of money and years of life? And is your solution the best one—or is it just the first one you thought of? Make sure you're honest with yourself about your answers.

Then, if you still feel you've identified a problem that you think you can solve, consider who might pay you to solve it. Is your product a good match for their needs?

It's also possible that no one will pay you to solve a problem you've identified. Hedberg Maps in Minneapolis, Minnesota, created an atlas of all the area sports facilities. The company thought that parents would want directions to the soccer fields and hockey rinks where young people were playing, and that school sports teams could sell the atlas as a fundraiser. However, parents were more comfortable getting directions from apps on their phones, and a local soccer association already had a lock on fundraiser sales. The map company ended up paying to have the unsold atlases destroyed.

If you've established that the problem in front of you is worth solving and potentially profitable, ask yourself: Who else has tried to solve it? Did that attempt work? What can you learn or borrow from other companies in the same industry? Don't disparage the competition. Most people aren't all that different from you—they, too, are trying their best to solve a problem. Instead of dismissing them, explain what's different about your solution and why it will be more successful.

At the end of the day, a prospective business owner needs to know if her idea is desirable, feasible, and viable. Is this a problem that should be solved? Will customers pay you enough for the solution to make solving the problem worth your while?

When you're answering these questions, don't make claims without backing them up with evidence. Keep your projections conservative, and be realistic about the time and resources available to you. It's good to be optimistic—that's why you're getting into business—but overly optimistic assumptions will set you up for failure. Whether you're building a house or a business, most things cost more and take longer than you initially predict. Write up a business plan that assumes the worst-case scenario. That way, at the very least, you'll meet your baseline. Anything above it is a bonus.

Operations

Now that you've identified a problem and your solution, you'll have to go about actually producing your product or streamlining your service. You'll need materials and a way to manufacture what you're selling. What method will you use to make your product? What facilities and equipment will you use? Who will do the work, and what will their roles be? What processes will you put in place for production? Will you have an office? A store? Where will these things be located? Will you need to find or build new locations? When, where, and how will you do that?

Operations have been an issue for Zellee, a Hawaii-based company that makes a plant-based fruit snack. The concept started as a home kitchen recipe, but formulating a recipe for commercial success involved hiring a food chemist and a nutritional label attorney. Next, the firm found someone who could package the result in squeeze pouches. But the owners quickly recognized the manufacturer wasn't a good fit, so Zellee went through two more options before they solidified a good relationship with a manufacturing facility.

Lisa O'Kelly
Lisa O'Kelly is cofounder of Zéllee Organic, based in Maui, HI. The company makes an organic, plant-based fruit jel snack that uses konjac, a plant from East Asia, to gel the product, instead of gelatin.

Their troubles with manufacturers may be over, but Zellee is still working out supplier issues. On its last run, the company had difficulty sourcing peach puree, says co-owner Lisa O'Kelly. "Ingredient supplies can be dependent on the quality of the last harvest," she says.

In your business plan, you'll want to think through your operations as specifically as possible. The goal is to lay a good foundation for production and sales—as well as alternatives so you're prepared when you hit a bump in the road.

Lisa says you'll most likely need to find more than one supplier, and you should talk to other businesses in the same space about your manufacturing options. If you're producing at a large scale, for example, you'll have many more variables to consider. "You may need to manufacture overseas, at least to start, because it's so much less expensive," she said. "US Department of Commerce Export Assistance Centers, which have feet on the ground all over, can help you figure out manufacturing and understand the questions and expenses involved."

For more on operations, check out Chapter 4.

Finances

Once you know how you'll source your materials and have developed the process you'll use to transform them into a finished product, you need to identify each of your costs. You should understand exactly how much you will spend to make a unit of whatever you're selling.

Without understanding how much it costs you to produce something, you can't know how much you need to sell it for in order to make a profit—or at least stay in business. "If you have a business where it costs you $100 to make an item and you can only sell it for $90, then you might as well just create an organization that gives $10 to every person you meet," Minnesota State's Yvonne Cariveau says.

Say you make muffins, and it costs you more to create them than you can charge for them: you don't have a business—you have a charity. Go look at the competition and see how much they're charging for a muffin. This is called benchmarking data, and in most industries, you can find prices for any given good by being curious and shopping as a customer. "Data is knowledge," Lisa says, "and it helps you make a structured guess. You can have the best muffins ever, and the numbers are still more important."

How many muffins do you think you can sell? Start with the total size of your market and figure out how many people you can make aware of your business through marketing. Of those who know about you, maybe between 2 and 3 percent will visit your website. An even smaller proportion will make a purchase. From playing with these numbers, you can create cash flow and balance sheet projections.

As you go forward, simultaneously try to increase income and decrease costs. Could you charge a little bit more? At what price point will a customer stop buying? "Get a projection sheet and play with the projections," Lisa says. "There are templates everywhere."

Remember, too, that you don't just need enough money to open. You need enough money to get through the inevitable ups and downs of the first few weeks and months. Most businesses aren't immediately profitable, and all businesses go through booms and busts. Assume that you'll earn less and spend more than you initially imagined.

While making your business plan, you should also think through how you'll manage repayments to investors and lenders if necessary. Whether they take a hands-on role or operate as silent partners, every financial contributor wants to know when you will repay the investment or loan, and at what rate of return. It's typical for investors to want out in three to five years.

This is just a taste of what you'll want to consider when it comes to finances—to learn more, check out Chapter 5.

Marketing

Now that you've thought through your operations and financial viability, how will you find prospective customers and tell them about your value proposition?

Chapter 6 explores marketing strategies in more detail, but it isn't as simple as handing out some flyers. You'll want to tap into your network; build an online brand, including on social media; consider partnerships with other small businesses; and explore advertisements and earned media opportunities. Marketing is a constantly moving target— you'll always need to be looking for new ways to reach your audience.

And remember that you're not only marketing your company. You're marketing your individual products, and it's important to do that strategically. "Market the things with the largest profit margins first," Lisa says. That advice forces you to think about the cost to you of whatever you're selling.

You also need to think about the kind of sales you're making. It's easier to sell more to existing customers than to find new ones. How will your business find first-time clients? And how will it persuade them to stick around and buy from you again?

◆ ◆ ◆

Those are the primary sections of a written business plan—and the primary concepts to think deeply about, even if you're not writing the plan out formally. From here, you can use or tailor the plan for any audience you need. You might have a presentation for an investor; it wouldn't hurt to show a possible lender a well-thought-out business plan. It may be something you continue to refine among your leadership team. But even if you simply keep it in a folder on your computer and never look at it again, the work you've done will stay in your mind, and it will help form your strategy going forward.

Take It on the Road

Before you dive in headfirst, make sure to test your conclusions. "Make your product, take it somewhere small, and see if anyone wants it," says Lisa. It could be at a fair or on a street corner. It could be a trial run with a few potential clients. Based on that experience, what about your projections do you need to change?

Here's an important factor: pay attention to how much you enjoyed the experience. "Figure out if you even like to do this," she adds. "Maybe you'll hate it!"

If it's the latter, think long and hard about whether this idea is the right place for you to dedicate a lot of time. Most businesses probably won't be very successful if their founders aren't excited to do the work.

A Few More Planning Tips

As you write your business plan:

- **Have a vision.** Present your vision for what you believe you are building. A vision can be more future looking and optimistic about your goals. Be as clear-eyed as you can be in stating what you want to be.
- **Be logical.** Think like a banker or an investor for the concrete details, not like a dreamer.
- **Support your claims** with statistics, facts, and quotes from knowledgeable sources.
- **Don't discuss rumors.** Hearsay about your competitors doesn't belong in a business plan.
- **Avoid superlatives.** *Major, unique, the first, the only, the best, the most, unbelievable, amazing, terrific*—none of these words should have a place in your plan. In most instances, you can't back up these claims with data, because they are, at their core, opinions. There's no way, for instance, to prove that you have the best Mexican food in town. (You can, however, quote someone else saying that—a food reviewer, for instance—if it will add credibility.) There's also a very good chance that your product or service is not truly the first or unique. That's fine. The world has room for more than one vintner. Just be truthful in what you claim.
- **Be realistic.** Don't overestimate your financial projections or underestimate your time frames. Assume that your business will bring in half the revenue that seems reasonable and take twice the time you initially

estimate to get up and running. If you're able to bring in more money in less time, that's great. Make the surprises good ones.

- **Hire or contract with an accountant** or a financial expert to help you think through the financial side of your business. If you're writing a business plan for investors or lenders, ask the accountant to put your financial projections in the standard business format that your audience expects.
- **Don't send investors a gimmick.** They'll eat the cookies that you send, but the baked goods won't make them more likely to invest in your business. Investors want facts, not snacks.

Ask for Help

Whether you create a formal business plan or not, thinking through a proposed business is a lot of work. You don't have to hire someone with an MBA or pay consultants—not at first, anyway. You can get help, usually for free, from a wide variety of sources:

- The Small Business Administration (SBA) is often the quickest way to find free help. It funds small business development centers (SBDC), often hosted by large universities, which can help you one-on-one for as long as you need.
- Your local chamber of commerce likely has resources and relationships with advisors and business content.

- County and city governments, as well as local, state, and federal lawmakers, often offer grants to help small businesses.
- Retired people from your industry might be happy to coach you, or you could join a group of current entrepreneurs who meet regularly for advice and support. Chambers of commerce and SBDCs can help you find both.
- Workforce Investment Boards exist in every state. They help unemployed people find jobs and offer subsidies to business owners to hire an employee for three to six months. They may also offer subsidized employee training.
- Your own network. "Think about your friend group," says Jen Pratt, owner of Fresh Sunshine Flowers in Sandpoint, Idaho. "Who can help you? You don't have to do this on your own. You have an amazing support system already."

Jen Pratt

Jen Pratt owns Fresh Sunshine Flowers in Sandpoint, ID. She began her business by selling out of a box truck with a side window, back when food trucks were at their peak.

Questions to Consider

- Have you sketched out your business plan, including vision, operations, and financial needs? Books, online resources, and Small Business Administration (SBA) resources can all help you organize and refine your thinking.

- Can you succinctly articulate your business plan?

- What problem are you solving or need are you filling? Will someone pay you for your solution?

- What business tools or vendors do you need to get started? Do you know how much it will cost and what you'll need to do to get them on board?

- What milestones will you aim toward on your way to success?

SELF-MADE
BOSSES

Julie Newman

Ilana Wilensky

Mike Yardley

Michael Lassner

Nat Case

CHAPTER 3

Legal Matters

Julie Newman
Julie Newman is a
licensing executive
specializing in
art influencers,
designers, and
design-based
corporate and
cultural brands. Areas
of expertise include
consumer products
retail strategy,
brand strategy,
with strengths in
brand management,
international strategic
partnerships, and
creative brand
extensions.

Five years after starting Jewel Branding in Atlanta, Georgia, Julie Newman says she felt like a dairy farmer who needed to milk her cows every day: "I couldn't go away for a few days and know that everything would be fine."

That's why she decided to bring on a partner who could help make sales and run the business—and when she met Ilana Wilensky at an industry networking event, she knew she'd met her match. "I had a gut feeling that this would work well," Julie says.

At first, Ilana worked as Julie's employee. But, over time, the two developed their own areas of expertise: Ilana mastered sales, marketing, and public relations, while Julie focused on finance, operations, and processes. After a year,

Ilana Wilensky

Ilana Wilensky is president of Jewel Branding and Licensing in Atlanta, GA. Her agency represents designers and brands to license their trademarks and designs to manufacturers across a wide range of consumer products that are sold through retail channels.

Ilana came aboard as an official partner. She bought a third of the business, with an option to buy another 15 percent after three years. Together, she and Julie also own a software business, which merchandizes the technology they've developed to run Jewel Branding to the rest of the branding industry.

Though they say they get on so well that they haven't had to refer to their contract, the pair couldn't have become official partners without a written agreement.

While taking the time to write down how your business will operate might sound like busywork, that couldn't be further from the truth. Not all partnerships are going to run as smoothly as Julie and Ilana's. Sometimes roles will be less clear; sometimes you'll have multiple people with varying degrees of ownership; and sometimes you'll need to account for intellectual property, protect yourselves from liability, save money on taxes, or manage some other variable within your agreement.

In each of these cases, you'll have to answer a question, usually right when you begin your business: How are you going to structure your company?

In this chapter, we'll walk you through your options and discuss a few other legal matters you'll want to think through. While we are outlining the basics, do your own web research and follow up with an attorney so that you have a more detailed view of the pros and cons of each structure and how it applies to your personal situation.

Partnerships

SPECIALIST

A partnership is a legal arrangement that lets two or more people own and operate a business together, sharing in that company's profits and losses.

Building a strong partnership is an intentional act. Jeremy Weinberg, a partnership law expert in Short Hills, New Jersey, says potential partners should always take time to ask each other questions to make sure they're on the same page. These include:

Jeremy Weinberg
Jeremy Weinberg is a tax attorney currently residing in Short Hills, New Jersey. Jeremy specializes in the taxation of partnerships and similar pass-through entities. After spending 10+ years in private practice, Jeremy retired from the practice of law to start a travel company and is now his own self-made boss.

- What is your vision for this business? How do you see it evolving? How do you imagine your current and future roles?
- What will each of you put into this partnership? Contributions might include money, expertise, time, contacts, a rent-free spot in a garage—anything, really!
- How will you allocate partnership income and loss among partners? If you're putting equal amounts of money, time, and skills into the business, it might

make sense to apportion income and loss 50/50. If your contribution levels aren't the same, what's the right way to split the pie?

- How much of what you earn will go back into the business? How much will be distributed to each partner? On what schedule?
- If one partner dies, will that person's shares go to her heirs or to the company's other shareholders? Or will those circumstances trigger a company sale, with proceeds divided between each partner or heir?
- How will this partnership end? You might intend to sell the business, perhaps when it reaches a particular level of sales or profitability. You could plan to someday sell your interest in the partnership. If that happens, does the other partner get right of first refusal on the purchase? Can your partner veto your sale if she prefers not to work with the purchaser you've selected? Will one partner buy out the other at some point?

Although tax laws dictate certain requirements for partnerships, you have a lot of flexibility in determining the answer to most of these questions, Jeremy says. A partnership agreement can set out what you've already decided you'll do at various junctures, or it can describe the process you'll use to make those decisions when the time comes. A clear written agreement can significantly contribute to a partnership's success, because it forces both people to think through hard questions they otherwise might put off until it's too late.

Mike Yardley
Mike joined the army out of high school and used the GI Bill to learn auto mechanics. Mike worked for auto dealerships until 2005. He made the decision to work for independent auto shops and found he was better off working for himself, which he has been since 2009.

Sometimes, simple problems sink partnerships. Mike Yardley, a mechanic and owner of MYT Automotive in Columbia Falls, Montana, was part of a partnership that he recalls falling apart because the pair didn't discuss how much each of them would earn or how they would pay the rent. "The friendship didn't survive being around each other all the time, becoming a business, and surviving the lean times," Mike says.

In other situations, more complicated problems are to blame, as when Michael Lassner, CEO of Allied Steel Buildings in Fort Lauderdale, Florida, realized that he and his partner worked well together in the short term but had opposing long-term visions. In retrospect, he says, he didn't pick the right person for the company he wanted to build. Recognizing that from the get-go would have saved a lot of time and stress.

Other partnerships have floundered simply because the kitchen is bursting with cooks. More partners can mean more money and expertise, but it can also mean more opinions and more jostling for control.

Julie and Ilana are proud of the partnership—and the companies—they've built. But it hasn't happened on its own. Outside of the legal agreement they worked up together, their strong partnership also depends on daily practices. Here are a few of their tips:

Michael Lassner
Michael Lassner, president of Allied Steel Buildings, is disrupting the global steel construction industry. He believes success is created by modeling business strategies around client needs. Michael leads an international team of innovators who tirelessly work daily to deliver on the promise of clients first.

- **Divide responsibilities.** Respect that the other person is competent to handle the items on their plate.
- **Make big decisions together.**
- **Communicate.** "We talk every day," Julie says. "We need to be on the same page for ourselves and for our employees. We try to have a united front and handle things together."
- **Put ego aside.** Support each other and your employees by making sure everyone gets recognition for their contributions.
- **Collaborate.** "We're collaborative, and we've found that it doesn't work if we hire people who aren't," Ilana says.

After eight years, Ilana and Julie are friends as well as business partners. They socialize together outside work. Their husbands even like each other. "We're very lucky that this is such a strong partnership," Ilana says. "That doesn't happen all the time."

Corporate Structure

Whether you're going into business on your own or with a partner, one of the first legal decisions you'll make is figuring out the corporate structure you'll use.

Your corporate structure lays out your company's parameters, governing how you pay taxes, how you split ownership, and a few things you are and aren't able to do. There are a variety of possible incorporation types, each with its own advantages and drawbacks. We'll walk you through them here.

Sole Proprietorship

This is the simplest form of incorporation. You don't need any particular paperwork to incorporate as a sole proprietor, though you may need local licensing and/or a DBA—a document stating that you're "doing business"—to operate legally. In some states, business owners file DBAs with the state secretary of state. Others ask you to file a DBA at the city or county level. Google "where to file a DBA?" to find out what your state requires.

A sole proprietorship is what's called a pass-through entity: company profits are taxed once, as part of the owner's personal income. Owners don't need to submit a separate tax return for their businesses; instead, they add a Schedule C to their personal tax return. The potential downsides to sole proprietorship are that you're on the hook for any business liability or debt you incur—and just one person can own your company. But because they're so easy to set up, it can make sense to start out as one. After all, you can always move to a different corporate structure later.

Limited Liability Company (LLC)

An LLC is a little more complex than a sole proprietorship, but the hassle isn't huge; you just have to file some paperwork and pay some fees.

Nat Case
Nat Case is a cartographer and designer in Minneapolis, MN, where he is also co-owner of INCase LLC. His work includes maps for *National Geographic* magazine and atlases, interpretive landscape signs, and maps for a variety of scholarly publishers.

Nat Case, a cartographer in Minneapolis, Minnesota, says that it took him around two hours to register his partnership as an LLC. He searched "how to register an LLC in Minnesota," and the results helped him fill out a form at the Minnesota State Department and announce the company's incorporation, which is a state requirement. The registration fee was less than $100, he says, and the public announcement cost around $50. INCase LLC, which offers cartographic and editorial services, has to renew the registration every year, but that's free and easily accomplished online.

In exchange for that small effort, incorporating as an LLC offers you significant benefits. For starters, you can have as many owners as you like. And while it's similar to a sole proprietorship in that it's a pass-through entity, meaning that business profits are taxed just once, it also has the advantage of protecting the business owners from business liabilities.

"If you're a sole proprietor, your personal liability is on the line if a customer or employee sues you," says Sarah Barrack, a partner at a New York law firm that she managed.

SPECIALIST

"You will pay any damages from your personal assets, which are all fair game."

But if you set up a legal corporate entity, such as an LLC, only your business assets are at risk. You're probably not going to lose your house or your retirement money, Andrew says.

Sarah Barrack
Sarah Barrack is a lawyer in the New York City metropolitan area. She has been working with small businesses and creators for decades. Sarah specializes in working with creative talent in the entertainment industry.

S Corporation

Like an LLC, an S corporation lets you have multiple owners—in this case, up to 100 shareholders, all of whom must be US citizens or residents. It keeps your personal and business liability separate, and profits are taxed just once. As with an LLC, you'll need to file paperwork and pay fees to stay in compliance. Structuring your business as an S corp also means that you'll have a board of directors, and you'll have to follow rules about holding meetings and keeping records. You'll need an attorney to help you set up an S corp.

LLCs and S corporations are both taxed once, on owners' personal tax returns, and they both protect owners' personal assets from business liability. S corporations do have some advantages over LLCs. Some investors prefer to put money into S corps, and because they've been around much longer than LLCs, S corps are often more familiar to lawyers and other advisors.

S corps also offer business owners the ability to receive both salary and dividends, which can mean a lower overall tax bill. LLC owners, by contrast, pay self-employment taxes, which can mean higher overall taxes.

If you hope to eventually raise capital by selling shares or going public, you'll want to incorporate as a C corporation. Changing from S corp to C corp status is easy and simple. The trip from LLC to C corp, on the other hand, is much more complex.

C Corporation

If you hope to one day sell your shares publicly, this is the best corporate structure for you. It allows unlimited shareholders and permits multiple types of stock shares. Otherwise, it's just like an S corporation, but with one significant difference: profits are taxed twice—first at the business level and then again at the personal level.

A C corporation structure might give you more access to capital, but at the price of reduced control for the initial owners, plus many more reporting requirements.

Like an S corp, a C corp is not a do-it-yourself project. You'll need an attorney with experience in this area.

"For small businesses owned by individuals, an S corp is a good choice, and an LLC is better," Sarah says. "You want a pass-through entity, one that is taxed as though it's just you, and taxed just once."

Unless you have a specific reason to choose a C corp construction, don't. An LLC and an S corp both protect you from personal liability without increasing your tax burden.

Making It Official

If you alone own your company, or you have a single partner, you may be able to do your own paperwork. You can also hire a service or a small business attorney. If you have multiple investors, Sarah recommends bringing a lawyer on board. Even in a two-person partnership, you should discuss what rights and responsibilities you'll each have, and document your agreement, in addition to the rights that any investors may have.

As you designate ownership, keep in mind that a business that is majority-owned by women or Black, indigenous, or other people of color will have advantages in marketing, landing government contracts, and potential eligibility for government programs, grants, and tax incentives. In a two-person partnership where one person is male and the other female, or one person white and the other an underrepresented minority, it may make sense to structure ownership not in exactly equal halves, but with a tilt to qualifying for this unique status. "My wife is my LLC partner, and if I'd been smart, I would have registered the company as more hers than mine," Nat Case says.

Licenses, Intellectual Property, Insurance, Privacy Protection, and Taxes

Filing paperwork to document your incorporation is just the beginning for many businesses. You may also need a license from your state or city. Research this, register, and pay fees as necessary. Yes, it's a hassle, but it's preferable to paying fines or even having your business shut down later if you ignore this step.

Look into other requirements, too. In general, if you want to start a business that involves safety precautions, such as food service, construction building systems repair, or haircutting, you are going to need to do more than simply register with your city to open up. Businesses that serve alcohol or involve firearms have both federal and state requirements. Google searches, professional organizations, and consultants can all help you navigate the thicket, too.

Pay attention to the legal side of any intellectual property you're using. If you're building a business using other people's technology, make sure you have permission to do so. You don't want to accidentally infringe on someone else's rights and have to dismantle your company. You should also protect your own intellectual property by filing for patents and copyrights as appropriate. A trade or intellectual property lawyer can help you with both research and the filing process.

Pick a business name and create marketing materials that don't copy anyone else, even accidentally. See what businesses are in the same space. Search online. When you incorporate, most states will let you search their database of company names. Do that so you don't rip off anyone else's name; that can come back to bite you, too.

No one wants to pay for insurance, but it's still important to do so. You'll want owner's or renter's insurance for your company's physical location, as well as errors and omissions (E&O) insurance to cover your liabilities. An insurance broker can provide a package that covers typical small-business exposures.

If you take information from your customers—email addresses, credit card details, account passwords, other private financial or personal information—you need to be sure that you protect that information from hackers. That means segregating information and shielding it electronically and manually in ways that comply with state and federal regulations. Choose technology products that protect customer information.

Don't overcomplicate things. Buy what you need now—and nothing more. Don't buy an enterprise software system for a one-person operation.

Another tip: Pay your payroll taxes, sales tax remittance, and estimated quarterly taxes on time. The penalties for not doing so aren't terrible, but they're also a completely unnecessary expense. It's very easy to get behind and never catch up if you don't stay abreast of your tax responsibilities. Helping you with this is one of your accountant's primary duties.

Franchises

You might purchase a franchise, or you might ultimately decide to turn your new business into a franchise.

There are multiple types of franchises: product franchises, manufacturing franchises, or business format franchises.

To franchise your business or become a franchisee, you'll want the help of an attorney with specific experience in this area.

◆ ◆ ◆

Unless you're opening up a law firm, odds are good that you aren't starting your business to do legal work. When you're busy, it's the last thing you're going to want to do, but it's also the only way you can be sure that your company is aboveboard. So, think about the type of business you want to form, research what kind of incorporation makes most sense for you, and get it done. You don't have time to waste. You have a business to start.

One last note: If you're worried you're in over your head figuring these things out, or you think you're at risk of skirting the law, hire a lawyer. It may feel expensive, but the peace of mind will be worth it.

Questions to Consider

- Do you want to start your business by yourself— or will you want a partner? If you do, what kind of partner do you want?

- How will you structure your business? Have you compared legal structures that fit your needs?

- Do you want many shareholders—or, eventually, to become public? Do you want to become a franchise?

- Are you covering all your bases on licensing, incorporation and set-up?

SELF-MADE
BOSSES

Peter Stein

Jonathan Sciabica

LaTonia Cokely

Lisa O'Kelly

Aylon Pesso

CHAPTER 4

Operations and Logistics

How to Get Up and Running

In 2015, Peter Stein was a man who loved oysters.

In 2016, Peter was a man who loved oysters and had a plan to make a living by farming them.

By early 2020, Peter had 2 million oysters in the water and was selling them to New York's top restaurants, where patrons ordered them nearly as fast as he could grow them—as though each one contained a pearl.

In half a decade, Peter went from being a fan of oysters to a man selling them hand over fist. How did he do it?

Sure, a big part of the reason for Peter's success is that his oysters are delicious; if they weren't, no one would buy

Peter Stein
Peter Stein owns Peeko Oysters, which is on Long Island near New Suffolk, NY. He can't remember a time when he didn't love oysters.

them. Ultimately, however, the reason Peter's business is so successful is that he pays close attention to every aspect of his operations.

Whether he's figuring out the best place to source baby oysters, refining his process to grow them into adulthood, or marketing to the restaurants that will ultimately serve them on plates of crushed ice or in bowls of creamy chowder, Peter has his business down to a science.

If you want to boost your margins, you'll want to think about operations the way Peter does. That's what we'll focus on in this chapter. Thinking through the processes and mechanics that make your company run is the difference between customers leaving your store happy and customers grumbling while they stand in a line that never seems to move. It's the difference between razor-thin margins and more comfortable margins. It's the difference between your company becoming a hobby that fades or a business that lasts.

Nailing down your operations—making sure your company is efficient and effective—will also make it possible for someone else to run your business. That's handy when you want to take a day off . . . or, one day, sell the company and retire or move on to something else.

Make the Thing You Make

Operations is about how your company gets from an idea to a finished product or service that it can sell to customers.

"Operations is essentially process management," says Lisa Skluzacek, operations manager for Nature Valley

Innovation at General Mills in Golden Valley, Minnesota. "You figure out your target customer and look at how you will get every item on your business menu into that person's hands."

Under the umbrella of operations, you'll find logistics, sourcing materials, inventory management, distribution, and sales processes. Within each category, you'll also find yourself asking all sorts of questions.

"If you're moving things in and out of your warehouse, how many loading docks do you need? If you're delivering bread, how many trucks and drivers do you need? Do you have enough cold storage for the butter? What's your timing on all of this?" Lisa says.

She adds that many small companies don't consider these business dynamics enough. "They just do it," she says. "But if you're going to grow your business, you need to think about how your jobs break down into component pieces, so that more people can do those jobs."

As a small business owner, you want every step of the process to run as efficiently as possible. That means you've got to get down to the nitty-gritty details.

SPECIALIST

Lisa Skluzacek
Lisa Skluzacek is operations business manager for snacks at General Mills' snack division in Golden Valley, MN. She has worked for General Mills since 1991 and is also an avid sailor and farmer.

Use Data to Design an Efficient Workflow

Whether you're a sole proprietor or leading a staff of dozens, spend time observing and refining your work process. Standardize the things you routinely do, and document your system. That way, if something in your process goes awry or feels inefficient, it will be easier to identify the problem and test new solutions, rather than having to reinvent the wheel every day.

Sometimes, your eyes will fool you. When you can, gather actual data and then use that data to make intelligent changes. Are there ways to improve trouble areas? Look at the step before and the step following a problem to get a broader perspective. Look for bottlenecks, too. For instance, maybe you're spending a lot of time managing your inventory. In that case, an automated inventory management system might save you time; it could also save you a lot of money.

Information can also help you improve your product. At Sciabica Family California Olive Oil & Gourmet Foods in Modesto, California, Jonathan Sciabica found that exchanging tall, thin bottles for shorter, squarer models both streamlined shipping and made the oil more practical for consumers to use. Why? Because the old bottles didn't fit on most kitchen shelves. The new ones do.

Jonathan Sciabica
Jonathan Sciabica runs Sciabica Family California Olive Oil & Gourmet Foods. His grandfather and great-grandfather began the business using knowledge they brought with them from Italy.

The old bottles didn't mail in standard-size boxes. The new ones do. Sometimes it's that simple.

Consider how you'll manage variability. Every business has slow days and weeks, as well as times when they're virtually "on fire" with orders coming in. How will you handle those surges and declines in demand?

Drafting a clear workflow makes training employees easier, because you'll know exactly what they should be doing, and they can go back and read it over if they need a reminder. It also makes it easier for employees to step in and take your place, temporarily or permanently, if you need to take a vacation or want to retire.

Hold meetings to talk about how your team is functioning. What's working? What could be better? Don't just talk; listen to their ideas, too. These meetings shouldn't be about pointing fingers, but about ironing out the kinks in your process.

Source Raw Materials

Every business that sells a tangible product needs raw materials. For Peter Stein, that includes space in the bay, called "bay bottom," and baby oysters. He's put a lot of thought into how he sources both.

There are two ways to grow oysters in New York: you either own bay bottom or you lease bay bottom from the county. Leasing requires less up-front money than buying, but it requires much more patience. Peter works in Suffolk

County, which holds just one annual lottery for 10-year leases on 60 ten-acre oyster-farming sites.

Alternatively, you could buy bay bottom. That's what Peter decided to do, purchasing his property from an oyster farmer who was leaving the industry. He could have gotten financing to help build out his operations, he says, but chose to avoid debt by paying cash from his savings.

Owning bay bottom was just the first step. Peter still had to go through an extensive permitting process with the Army Corps of Engineers, the Department of Environmental Conservation, the town of Southold, the Coast Guard, and Suffolk County. "You're putting things in the water that could be a navigational hazard, so that's why the Coast Guard cares," Peter says. "The US Corps of Engineers gets involved because you're putting things in the water that could disintegrate."

Peter navigated the permitting process on his own, without help from a lawyer. But depending on the complexity of the process and your expertise in the industry—as well as time and money constraints—you may choose to bring a lawyer in to help, and that's fine, too. "There's no playbook for this," Peter says. "Anyone who starts a business needs a certain kind of grit and persistence. In food production, you bring that to another level. You're producing something that people are going to consume, so food producers are more heavily regulated and scrutinized by governmental agencies."

Peter adds that he was pretty sure he could create a viable business around oysters, and that optimism kept him going as he slogged through the permitting process.

"I know a lot of people in the restaurant business in New York City, so I never doubted that there was a market and I could access it," he says.

Once you know what your raw materials will be, you need reliable ways to source them. With access to bay bottom and permits in place, Peter needed baby oysters and oyster hotels for them to live in and grow. The oyster hotels use a tray system, with trays made of steel mesh. Peter decided not to build the cages himself. "I could have learned to weld, but it's more efficient to let other people assemble our cages," he says. "My time is more valuably spent selling oysters to top restaurants."

In nature, baby oysters, also called oyster seeds, float around for two weeks, then latch onto a surface in the bay and start growing. Stein buys his oyster seeds when they've already grown substantially, because it means his process will require less labor—and the oysters are more likely to survive.

"You pay more, but you have less labor and mortality, plus the oysters are easier to handle, because they're bigger," Peter says. "How much time do you have to wait? How much labor are you willing to put in? Those are questions you have to answer."

Find the Right Suppliers

There aren't many oyster hatcheries on the East Coast, and not every hatchery sells oysters at the bigger size Peter prefers. That narrows his choices. He also has to think about transportation. "Going to Maine means two days of travel time, so I like hatcheries that are closer to me and don't require a truck, a trailer, or a very expensive UPS bill," he says.

Peter tracks the performance of oyster seeds from different hatcheries to help him decide if paying more or using hatcheries that are farther away makes sense for his bottom line. That's how he decided against driving to buy oyster seeds from an attractive hatchery in Cape Cod, Massachusetts. "They're more expensive and they aren't materially better," he says. "Why pay 20 percent more?"

Over the past four years, Peter has used five or six different hatcheries. He's continuing to refine his opinions about which of those offer the best value.

LaTonia Cokely
LaTonia Cokely owns Adjourn Teahouse in the Washington, DC, metro area. She wanted a tea and wellness brand for years and started Adjourn when her husband gifted her the incorporation details for Christmas.

Another small business owner, LaTonia Cokely, who runs Adjourn Teahouse in Washington, DC, also works to track down the right suppliers for the tea blends she creates. "I do a lot of research for my supply chain," LaTonia says. "I belong to a network of similar businesses where I can talk with owners and connect with their distributors."

That strategy has connected LaTonia with five different herb sellers, but she prefers to buy directly from farms. They tend to have the sustainably sourced, organic options her customers prefer. Expense, availability, and consistency also matter to her—and to the people who buy her products.

It's not possible to get every ingredient for each of LaTonia's teas all year round—a problem she solves by offering both signature teas, which have readily available ingredients, and limited editions, which have ingredients that are more difficult to find. "I'm always looking for additional possible suppliers," she says.

Manage Inventory

Peter started his business with three oyster hotels. Now, he has about 130. That's around 2 million oysters in the water, all of which need regular inspections for growth rate and disease.

To keep track of his inventory, Peter knew he would need software. At first, he tried to build it himself, coding a product that would geo tag oyster hotel locations through his cell phone. But, before long, he joined forces with someone who was creating similar software, becoming a beta tester. "It's easier to tweak existing software than to build it from the ground up," he says.

He's working to make his OysterTracker software 100 percent accurate, but Peter says that he can't let perfect be the enemy of good. "I'll take 80 percent accurate today over 100 percent accurate three months from now," he says.

Oysters grow during the summer months and are dormant through the winter, so it's up to Peter to make sure that he's balancing supply and demand throughout the year.

"Software helps me keep track of that inventory," he says. "If I'm selling 10,000 oysters a week and I have 30,000 oysters in the bay, I know I'll be out of oysters by the new year. Or, if I have 300,000 oysters in the bay, I need to get a giddyap on my sales, or I won't have room for the next batch of oysters."

In addition to planning his sales, Peter needs to anticipate his needs for staff and gear. He has a boat and a minicrane system, in addition to the oyster hotels, which all cost money. Year-round, he has two full-time employees, but during the summer, he hires part-timers as well. "I get data and I plan accordingly," he says.

Get Your Manufacturing Process Right

Peter's manufacturing process involves leaving oyster seeds in the bay and waiting while the oysters grow themselves—for the most part. He also runs the growing oysters through a tumbler every three to six weeks during the summer growing season. Bouncing around in the tumbler, which looks like a giant bingo cage, chips off shell length and encourages the oyster to put energy into growing a deeper, harder shell. "It's a little like pruning a plant," Stein says.

For many other firms, manufacturing is more complicated. Zellee Organic, a snack business based in Hawaii and Northern California, started with a family recipe. But the owners quickly realized that there's a big difference between a recipe that makes enough for four or five people and one that makes thousands of servings. "I spent hours and hours making various recipes," says co-owner

Lisa O'Kelly. "Once we were happy with our formulation on the stovetop, our contractor food scientist helped convert the measurements to the batch requirements. We did many test runs as well at the co-packer."

Lisa O'Kelly
Lisa O'Kelly is cofounder of Zellee Organic, based in Maui, HI. The company makes an organic, plant-based fruit jel snack that uses konjac, a plant from East Asia, to gel the product, instead of gelatin.

Like Zellee, you'll also need to choose how you'll package your product, which can be easier said than done. At first, Zellee couldn't find anyone to produce squeeze pouches, since manufacturers in the United States sometimes required minimum orders of millions of packages. "We were a small startup and didn't have the capital to meet the minimum requirements," Lisa says.

But Zellee eventually found a plant in California that had squeeze pouch equipment left over from another client and was willing to try a run of 30,000 pouches. They couldn't find a plant that was willing to do small production runs, so Zellee next tried a plant in Utah. "That experience wasn't great," Lisa says. "They were also new and there were a lot of hiccups. Along the way, we should have talked to the factory's other clients. If you look at other companies' packaging, you can get a good sense of where it's made. Call them up and ask if they're happy, or ask the packager to offer references."

Zellee has since moved to a larger, more established packager, which has enabled it to increase production runs with confidence.

It's important to have mutual trust with your co-packer. "As with most things, having strong, honest relationships with your partners is a must," Lisa says. "You grow together."

Optimize Your Distribution Plan

For Jonathan Sciabica, owner of Sciabica Family California Olive Oil & Gourmet Foods, packaging and distribution go hand in hand. It started with Jonathan's realization that he needed to get his product to online purchasers more quickly. "People put olive oil on the grocery list when they run out," he says. "It was taking 10 days for us to get oil to retail customers, and by then, they'd have bought something else."

Flat-rate boxes and padded envelopes from the post office came to the rescue. "The flat-rate padded envelope has changed our business," Jonathan says. "The post office rep drops off pallets of boxes and padded envelopes, and then they pick them up, filled with bottles of olive oil." The orders usually reach customers in just two or three days, even in Alaska and Hawaii. (Delivery speed dropped during the Covid-19 pandemic in 2020 but rebounded in 2021.)

Next, Sciabica adjusted its bottles to fit better inside the boxes and padded envelopes. At the time, tall, thin bottles were in vogue. The company could get 250-milliliter bottles of this shape into a flat-rate box or envelope, but its 500-milliliter bottle didn't fit.

Sciabica redesigned its bottles to be shorter and broader. Now the company can fit two 500-milliliter bottles in a flat-rate padded envelope, and five bottles into the medium-sized flat-rate box. "Understanding how purchases happen and making the appropriate changes has let us offer Amazon-level service through the post office," Jonathan says.

The company made another helpful change when it began offering its product in a bag-in-box container, which uses plastic bags rather than bottles. Olive oil normally oxidizes after about three months in an open bottle. "It gets bland and starts to smell like crayons," Jonathan says. For that reason, the company wanted to get rid of its half-gallon jug.

The University of California at Davis released a study on the benefits of bag-in-box for olive oil, and Jonathan was intrigued. "Bag-in-box technology was associated with cheap wine, and that's unfortunate, because the packaging isn't cheap and it protects the wine better," he says. "Olive oil always gets used over time, so it makes even more sense to bag-in-box it."

Jonathan found a manufacturer that could handle making the bag, then had the box made locally and bought a machine to do the filling. "We created a product that you can use over six months with no oxidation," he says.

When it comes to distribution, you'll have a few choices to make, depending on the type of business you run. Sciabica distributes to online customers through the mail. Restaurants can use delivery services like DoorDash or Postmates. If you're distributing nationwide, you might use private distributors to deliver your products in bulk. Many small consumer brands are starting to use e-commerce platforms as distribution channels. They can drop-ship their products straight to a fulfillment center, never letting it sit in local inventory at all.

But for many businesses, outsourcing distribution isn't worth it. Peter Stein, for instance, strongly believes in selling directly to restaurants.

"No distributor cares more about my product than I do," he says.

He handles the deliveries himself and likes having individual relationships with the chefs and restaurant owners who buy his oysters. That, he says, is because purchasers are more likely to be loyal to someone they know, and he's able to fix any problems on the spot, by comping or replacing an entire order if something goes wrong.

Adjust as You Go

When considering your operations, it's important to realize that it may take you a while to get your systems in order. And as technology and software develop—not to mention as customer demands change—if you want to keep your business as efficient as possible, you'll need to keep revisiting your processes.

Zellee had a hard time finding the right manufacturing relationship, but, at times, it has also struggled to find raw materials, like organic peach puree. Its story isn't the exception. No matter what your company sells, there will be glitches and even outright breakdowns in your supply chain.

Sometimes, you may be able to solve minor problems by adjusting your offerings, as LaTonia Cokely does with her limited-edition teas. Nothing prevents you from hyping up hazelnut season, for instance, and driving demand by telling customers that they should buy now because they only have two weeks to enjoy this special flavor.

However, when a supply is critical to your business's functioning—flour for your bakery, hot dogs for your hot dog truck—you should always have a backup plan for securing it. Cultivate more than one source for the materials and services you need. If your plan A falls through, you need to be able to access another option immediately, or you may risk your ability to function at full capacity until you find a supplier.

"Get very familiar with your supply chain. Identify what's normal for your business, as well as what's within your control and what's outside your control," says Samantha Ku, who leads operations for Square's lending and banking business in San Francisco. "Prioritize the things that could actually close your business. Do you have a plan if that happens?"

Samantha Ku
Samantha Ku is the COO of Square Financial Services, Square's FDIC-insured bank. She runs a powerful operations team of well-trained credit experts.

Examine Your Sales Data

With your product ready to sell, your next task is to pay attention to your sales process and results, then make educated changes that improve your business.

Aylon Pesso and his father, Gidon Pesso, run Pesso's Ices & Ice Cream in Bayside, New York, where the younger

Aylon Pesso
Together with his father, Aylon Pesso owns and runs Pesso's Ices & Ice Cream in Bayside, New York. His favorite ice cream flavor is roasted marshmallow.

Pesso pays close attention to the flavors the shop sells and the hours, days, and months when it sells them.

"We adjusted our hours by looking at our hourly sales," Aylon says. "We didn't make any money until maybe two o'clock, so we moved our opening time later."

Tracking ingredient costs revealed that the price of making their ice cream had risen substantially between 2007 and 2011—but the shop hadn't raised prices for consumers. So Pesso did a full cost analysis and simplified the product line while also raising prices.

"We went from small, medium, and large to charging by number of scoops, and we started selling more of the smaller sizes. Very few people get four scoops. We got rid of the quart size, but kept pints, and we stopped doing egg creams, floats, and sodas," Aylon says. "Ice cream is more money and less work."

There were a few complaints from customers, but most ice cream fans didn't notice the changes, didn't care, or enjoyed the simpler menu. "I was less exhausted by choice and able to buy better ingredients, and we started making more of a profit," Aylon says.

When he advises other business owners, Aylon tells them to track first, then simplify. "I only started tracking our topping costs last month, and it turns out that I was losing money on some of them," he said. "I figured that they were cheap enough. Wrong. I've been losing money all this time on my M&Ms."

Look at everything: in Pesso's case, the cost of ingredients, spoons and napkins, overhead, even how he was spending his time. "Don't just look at things from your perspective," Aylon says. "Use data."

Aylon standardized and batched his processes after closely examining the amount of time he was spending on various tasks. "Don't do inventory five times a day. Take one day a week and inventory everything at once. Maybe implement an online inventory system," he says. "Have standard ways of doing things. Write out checklists. Don't memorize your recipes. Have a standard interview for employees, a standard job application. Go from reactive to predictive."

It may feel like these kinds of steps will make you busier than you already are, and that might be true for a few days or even a few weeks. But in the long term, it will bear fruit—or, perhaps, fruit sorbet. "It's like working out," Aylon says. "It sucks while you're doing it, and then it makes things so much better. You're already exhausted. If you do just a little bit more in a different way, you'll get a time refund."

That is true within every facet of your business, from sourcing raw materials to tracking your sales. The more you refine your processes, the more efficient you will be. That's why nailing down your operations couldn't be more important to your success.

Questions to Consider

- Where are the bottlenecks or weak points in your supply chain and in your workflow?

- What options do you have for raw materials, manufacturing, and distribution? Would your business benefit from outsourcing any of these processes—or bringing them back in-house?

- Any of the steps in your supply chain could break down. Which breakdowns would force you to close your business? Do you have a strategy for how to prevent that before it happens, or a backup plan if it does?

- Have you crunched the numbers? As billionaire entrepreneur Mike Bloomberg says, "In God we trust. Everyone else: bring data."

CHAPTER 5

Finances

How to Manage Your Money, Get Loans, and Get Paid

Growing up in Atlanta, Georgia, stylist Germanee G got a clear message about entrepreneurship: Don't do it. The potential freedom wasn't worth the financial risk.

"I was taught to find a good job and stay there," Germanee says.

With that understanding in her mind, leaving her job as a Gap corporate merchandiser to make her side hustle her full-time job was an especially frightening prospect for Germanee, who now splits her time between Atlanta and Los Angeles. "It's a big eye-opener to no longer have that corporate check," she says. "I had to learn how to monetize my passion, swiftly."

Germanee G
Bicoastal wardrobe stylist Germanee G provides branding solutions and wardrobe styling to some of the fiercest thought leaders, game changers, and trailblazers making waves in startups and Fortune 500 corporations.

Germanee wanted to be smart about her finances. So, before giving up on her corporate gig, she decided she would build a buffer of $30,000 in her bank account. "I was on a rigorous savings plan," she says. When she finally did quit her job, she knew she had enough saved up to cover six to nine months of rent and food if her business didn't initially meet her projections.

Now, three years into her role as a small business owner, Germanee continues to carefully monitor her finances. Sometimes she feels like she spends more time with QuickBooks than with her fiancé. She also works with an online bank designed for small businesses. Her Los Angeles apartment includes her studio space, so the business helps to pay her rent. She doesn't pay herself a salary yet, though she does take a manageable monthly allowance from her company. Any money she doesn't spend, she deposits into savings.

Which is all to say: Germanee thinks *a lot* about her finances—and if you want to run a small business, you should, too.

Thankfully, there are pressure-tested strategies that can help you prepare for whatever challenges—and opportunities—come your way. In this chapter, we'll show you how.

Start with the Basics

Think carefully about the kind of company you plan to start and the capital it will require. Some businesses—say, if you're an author, a graphic designer, or a social media marketer—might require little beyond a computer, a cell phone, and internet access. Others, like restaurants or other businesses with a physical location or inventory, will take substantially more money to set up before you open the doors to customers.

You can begin very small and grow incrementally, funding expenses from your own pocket. You don't need to begin with years' worth of expenses already in the bank.

You do, however, need to fund any legal requirements your business might have at the beginning. Go online and check state, county, and city websites to see what you'll need: a business license, permits to handle food, a license to cut hair, a taxi medallion, a liquor license. These all might require you to pay a fee.

There may be other requirements as well, like having a handwashing sink in a business that handles food. Get those things taken care of before you begin. If you operate without required facilities, you may be shut down, and there could be barriers to starting up again. Each industry has its own unique needs that take time to explore in detail.

A less dramatic path that you'll also want to avoid: you could simply waste a lot of time and money. Oakland, California, chef Leilani Baugh recalls that she spent $1,200 in fees on getting the wrong permits before finding out what her business

Leilani Baugh
Leilani Baugh owns Roux and Vine, a restaurant in Oakland, CA. She grew up with a love of food, learning Southern cooking from her Black grandmother and Chinese cooking from her Chinese grandmother.

actually required. Take a little extra time doing research and filling out the proper paperwork before you get started.

Don't Forget a Cash-Flow Cushion

No matter how your business operates, here's one thing that's nonnegotiable: You're going to need enough money to run your firm, make payroll, and keep yourself afloat between the day you begin the business and the day it starts supporting you. As part of making a business plan, you need to take an educated guess at how long that might be. Be realistic.

The more volatility you have in your business income, the more reserve you need in your account. If your business expenses go up—when you hire an employee, for instance—you need to add to your business reserve. A good rule of thumb is to have anywhere from six to nine months of your personal paycheck and ongoing business expenses saved up. Put it in the most flexible account possible—a checking or savings account works—so you can draw on it when you need it. It's your umbrella for a rainy day.

In general, your business will need three categories of money: (1) the money you'll need to run the business before it starts making money; (2) the amount you'll need to keep yourself running; and (3) your cushion—the amount you'll need to get through a rough patch in case money stops flowing. Whatever your estimate of this third number is, add a margin of error to it. Your margin of error should be developed by understanding your own risk tolerance and ability to manage your personal life if things don't work as planned. There will always be surprises, hiccups, and complexities you haven't considered. Once you've factored that in, you'll have your grand total: the amount of money you need to start your business.

That number may look daunting. But you might be able to reduce your startup costs by starting smaller: instead of starting an editorial services company, for instance, work as a freelance writer for a while and grow your business from there.

You could also put together a business over time while you still have a job working for someone else, and use that income to help fund your new operation. Of course, this plan has downsides, too. "That might seem like you're reducing your risk, because you still have an income, but it can drag things out—you might be taking a lot longer to get to opening day," says Ted Kosev, an expert who has worked with thousands of small businesses at Square and Amazon. One way or another, Kosev says, "you'll have to spend resources before you make money."

SPECIALIST

Ted Kosev
Ted Kosev built banking products at Amazon and Square. He moved into fintech after a long career as a banking executive.

As a prospective new business owner, you'll also need to sort out what form of incorporation you'll use, find a lawyer if you need one, and choose a bookkeeper or find an online bookkeeping solution.

According to Ted, before you crunch any of those numbers, you should do something far more basic—and far more important: "Try to boil your startup down to the simplest, most focused version, and from there, you can grow it or make it more complicated," he says. "Do people want to buy this good or service? You need the answer to that question as quickly as possible. Your livelihood depends on it."

Separate Business and Personal Finances

Many companies begin with the owner's personal and business finances entwined—and sole proprietorships often stay that way indefinitely.

SPECIALIST

Natalie Taylor

Natalie Taylor is a Certified Financial Planner™ in Santa Barbara, CA. Before starting her financial-planning firm, she spent eight years with Ameriprise, five years at LearnVest, and three years consulting in the fintech space.

But no matter what, Natalie Taylor, a Certified Financial Planner, consultant, and former executive at Ameriprise and LearnVest, says you will want to take the necessary steps to separate your own bank account from your business's.

If your corporate structure protects you from personal liability if things go wrong, separating personal and business finances is even more important.

"That's part of what gives you liability protection," Natalie says. "If you have an LLC but your accounts are in individual ownership rather than LLC ownership, you're less likely to have protection and more likely to have to argue about it in court if things get dicey."

One way to keep finances separate is to use different accounts for different purposes. That's what Ilana Wilensky, president of Jewel Branding and Licensing in Atlanta, does. "You need to keep things as separate as possible," she says. "That helps you manage your accounting, understand your income and expenses, and keep track of your tax write-offs.

"We've created different accounts within our business account, which helps us set aside money for payroll and expenses," Ilana adds. The company has accounts for income, checking, and operating expenses, plus an account that holds money that's owed to clients.

Ilana Wilensky
Ilana Wilensky is president of Jewel Branding and Licensing in Atlanta, GA. Her agency represents designers and brands to license their trademarks and designs to manufacturers across a wide range of consumer products that are sold through retail channels.

"We also have a profits account," Ilana says. "We try to set aside money there to build a little profit, and sometimes, we give ourselves a distribution at the end of the year."

Business accounts are a way to organize yourself when you are running a business. They're also simply a sound practice. If your business money is in a personal account, Natalie says, it's hard to get a good sense of how much money a business is earning or spending, and it complicates taxes and credit. "Separating your business finances helps you figure out whether or not you're profitable and makes it much easier to track deductible business expenses. It also lets you put some distance between your business's income fluctuations and your personal household finances," she adds.

A bank account also helps businesses prove consistent revenue, should they ever want to apply for a loan. Licenses and tax returns help start the clock on securing a loan, too. Because so many small businesses fail in the first year, showing the financial evolution over time will help you establish credibility with banks and other potential lenders.

Put Yourself on Payroll

Many business owners don't earn enough to pay themselves as they work to get their new ventures off the ground. But, if everything works out, there *will* come a day when your company is the source of your income. When that day comes, here's an important tip: Don't just transfer profits to your personal bank account. Pay yourself a monthly salary.

Ilana says that she and her business partner pay themselves a monthly salary, though the amount changes every year. "As soon as you're able, allocate money to pay yourself. Then schedule paying yourself—or you will always be the last priority," she says. "Get in that habit. It can be easy to not do it." Another way to establish peace of mind, according to Natalie, is to give yourself a bonus whenever your business has a good quarter. Alternatively, she says, if your business's cash flow is less consistent, you can space your bonuses out so they come every six months or once a year.

Bonuses aside, Natalie says that, in general, "your business fluctuations shouldn't affect your personal finances, so you should have an emergency fund inside your business, as well as a personal emergency fund."

Natalie advises, "Having a cash reserve within your business gives you the ability to pay yourself a regular paycheck each month, regardless of whether business income is up or down in any particular month. A steady paycheck enables you to cover your personal expenses, like your mortgage, food, and other bills, without worrying about whether your business had a good month or not." If you already have a personal accountant you like to work with, it's fine to ask that person to work as your business accountant, too, especially if you will begin as a sole proprietor. Keeping a familiar face around for the short term doesn't mean you can't hire a new accountant if your needs change.

Get a Bookkeeper

Once your business has money, you need to keep track of it, because understanding how money enters and exits your business is at the heart of understanding your firm.

Unfortunately, many business owners see bookkeeping as a chore, a matter they will deal with later—next week, next year. Unless you've specifically started a bookkeeping firm, crunching numbers is probably not your expertise.

That's precisely why, sooner or later, you will almost certainly need a bookkeeper. According to Kurt Rathmann, an entrepreneur, investor, advisor, and CPA in Austin, Texas, many business owners start off doing the books themselves, usually with software: "It's fine to go through the phase where you do the bookkeeping yourself as a way of understanding the business."

SPECIALIST

Kurt Rathmann
Kurt Rathmann is an entrepreneur, investor, advisor, and CPA in Austin, TX. He says that if you aren't in the bookkeeping business, you should probably let someone else handle that function at your company.

What's not okay, Kurt says, is to hang onto managing the bookkeeping forever as part of your daily responsibilities, costing you time spent doing things that generate revenue. "When the bookkeeping is an opportunity cost keeping you from doing more important things, you need to hire help," he says.

Bookkeeping also isn't a chore that you should be worrying about when the alternative is spending time with your family or friends. After all, finding someone to crunch your numbers isn't expensive—and doing so not only saves you hours but also spares you the nagging sensation that there is always something you should be doing. It's also an option, he says, to launch your business with a bookkeeper in place—allowing you to take advantage of that person's knowledge in setting up your back office and readying you for future growth. This option, if you can manage it financially, should give you peace of mind as well.

According to Kurt, you can find a quality bookkeeper through online marketplaces and networks, including QuickBooks. Word of mouth is a good option, too. Either way, he says, you want someone who is tech forward and can get you up and running on modern software that helps give you visibility into your accounts and business trends.

"Lots of shops use old technology, with owners looking to retire soon," he says. "The technology space around small businesses will evolve even more quickly in the next five years, and you want information at your fingertips. The virtual nature of back-office solutions will be ever more important."

In addition to helping you understand and make strategic decisions about your business, a good bookkeeper can also make sure you are prepared to apply for a loan.

Kurt recalls a pair of brothers he knew who owned a coffee shop and went to Nicaragua every year to buy coffee beans. "One year the traveling brother bought way too many coffee beans, and it sent the business into an unhappy spiral," he says. "Too much inventory meant they couldn't make payroll, and the whole thing went from there, with a lot of interpersonal conflict between the brothers. A loan of $8,000 would have seen them through. They've since recovered, but it didn't need to be nearly so painful." A tech-savvy bookkeeper could have ensured that the business was ready to apply for that loan and even pointed out that this was a viable solution to the problem.

Of course, we understand that it's not always easy to identify savvy bookkeepers before you've worked with them. So here are a few suggestions on going about hiring the right person for your business.

Certified public accountants (CPA) pass a rigorous exam for their certifications, so they're typically more expensive than less-credentialed bookkeepers. Your business doesn't necessarily need a CPA. "You're looking for someone who is qualified to do the work and eager about your business," Kurt says. "You might still have a CPA in your life during tax time or as an annual check-in. You may evolve into needing a CPA."

Ask a potential bookkeeper:

- What processes would you recommend putting in place? For instance, if I run a business that's appointment-based, should I send out an invoice at every appointment or wait until the end of a day, week, or month? What's the easiest way to minimize the steps to getting paid on time?
- Will your system be one that another bookkeeper could inherit? It's common for businesses to outgrow their bookkeepers, Kurt says, and to move along to another professional who has the skills they've evolved into needing. You might end up with more than one bookkeeper, each handling a distinct portion of your needs.
- Will you also help me with payroll, bill pay, W-2 and 1099 forms, tax preparation, and strategic advisory work?
- What are you best at? What isn't your strong suit? Everyone has strengths and weaknesses, and potential bookkeepers should be honest with you about theirs. After all, it makes a big difference whether the thing they're bad at is something you do or don't need.
- May I talk with customer references? Try to talk with both customers who have had good experiences with the bookkeeper and clients who have had less successful relationships.

Once you've found a bookkeeper you want to hire, take an active role in making that person successful. Get into a rhythm of checking in weekly. It will help keep you disciplined and proactively ready for both problems and opportunities, and it will save you time in the long run.

A weekly appointment will also help make sure that you get your bookkeeper the necessary data and paperwork. Most bookkeepers spend at least half their time chasing clients down, trying to get the information that they need to do their jobs. Don't be that person who always needs reminders; besides being respectful, it could make a difference for your bottom line, too.

"If you're not irritating and constantly creating additional work for your bookkeeper, you get to be an appreciated customer, and you'll get more attention and service," Kurt says. It's another way of saying, being a good client can help create a better relationship between you and your bookkeeper.

Beyond that regular check-in and getting your bookkeeper the material she needs, try not to be a control freak. She's a professional; give her room to work. That's the reason you hired her in the first place.

"If you can't do that," Kurt says, "you don't have the right person. Value their expertise. This should not be a contentious relationship. You need to be able to trust this person."

Choose a Business Bank

Look for the same qualities in a business bank that you'd look for in your personal bank: low and easily understood fees, a good online interface, account minimums that you can meet, apps that let you make transactions remotely, and a no-fee credit card. (Another tip: That credit card can also help you stay organized. Use one credit or debit card for business expenses and pay it from your business account. When it's time to pay taxes, the statements will give you a ready-made list of deductible business expenses.)

There are other things you might want from your banking relationship, too. Will you need to go to the bank branch, maybe to deposit cash that your business generates? In that case, it might make sense to choose a bank that has a nearby physical office.

It could also make sense to pay attention to the way a bank bundles its offerings, including checking, savings, bill pay, and credit. What administrative support will the bank offer you? Are there minimum account balances? Will the bank automatically charge you for things you probably won't use? How high are the fees for things you will use?

Most banks, especially online, are happy for you to have multiple accounts, though some brick-and-mortar banks levy fees for business accounts and have minimum balance requirements. Regardless of the cost, you'll need to pony up the cash for at least two: a checking account and a savings account where you keep your money to pay taxes.

Beyond that, Natalie Taylor suggests sticking with the number of accounts you really need, and no more. A simple structure, she says, "is easiest to maintain long-term, and it's also the easiest to scale."

As you're looking at options, you should consider using an online bank, since those often charge lower fees and have more convenient remote capabilities than offline ones. Found, Square, Brex, and Mercury are all online business banking options—and by the time this book is in your hands, there will likely be many more. Each has a different focus and some also specialize by industry or business type. Online banks can be terrific partners, but if you make frequent cash deposits or withdrawals, or an online bank makes it more difficult to move your money between your personal and business accounts, you should be realistic about whether the lower fees and better interfaces will be worth it for you.

Don't forget to look at credit unions and community banks, as well. Credit unions exist to serve their membership, which means that sometimes they're able to take more time with complicated clients.

Ilana Wilensky says that she and her partner chose to work with a smaller bank because it charges lower fees than its competition, and because they could develop a stronger bond with their banker. "There was tremendous value in having a relationship with a banker," she says. "The big banks wouldn't give us the time of day. If you need help with financing and you can find a personal relationship with a banker, it definitely helps."

That was certainly true for Ilana. After years of developing their relationship with their bank, her company, Jewel Branding, was able to receive a Small Business Administration (SBA) loan through her local bank.

Begin a
Business-Banking Relationship

As Ilana learned, a bank doesn't just hold onto your money—it can be a key partner in your growth. So don't wait until you need money to begin the process of building a relationship with your bank, and definitely don't start with the lending side of the bank.

Instead, start with the basics you need to run your business. Collect information about lending and other business products when you open the account, but keep in mind that the bank probably won't lend to anyone with fewer than two years in business. This isn't a steadfast rule, so do your homework and look for options.

In the meantime, try your best to build trusting relationships. Make business purchases and deposits through the account, since that kind of activity will inspire confidence. Most banks will also be impressed if your personal finances are in good standing, including your personal credit score, which is why it could be smart to do your personal banking at the same institution as your business banking.

Because of laws designed to combat money laundering, your bank has a legal obligation to know who owns your business, what kind of business it is, how you get paid, and by whom. What form of incorporation do you have? Do you plan to make frequent cash deposits? These are the kinds of questions banks will be asking.

Don't be tempted to skirt the truth about what your business does. Be transparent with your bankers. Every large deposit—$10,000 and up under federal law, but potentially as little as $5,000—will be flagged for a deeper review. Bankers aren't stupid. They'll figure it out if you're trying to skirt the rules. When they do, they will close your account. They may also file a "suspicious activity report" and put you on a list that will keep other legitimate banks from accepting you as a customer. "Don't get started in a shady way; get your business licenses and whatever else you need to operate properly," Ted Kosev advises. "If you don't, it will come back to haunt you when you need to establish banking relationships or other vendor relationships."

Even if your business is not on a bank's list of higher-risk industries, there may be other factors that make finding a bank more difficult. For instance, perhaps you have a trust in your name for estate-planning reasons, which you would like to use to open your business. That is completely above board, but because trusts involve multiple legal entities and can be used to blur sources of funds, it means taking you on as a client will force a bank to do more work. For that reason, a bank may turn you down.

Don't Be Afraid to Invest in Your Business with a Loan

Saving up the money you need to start your business is an option, of course, as is funding as you go or using crowdsourcing, an inheritance, a severance package, or another windfall. Some entrepreneurs have gotten grants to start businesses, though these are often difficult to come by.

It's much more common to launch a business with at least some amount of debt. Often that debt comes from credit cards; loans from friends and family are also typical, as are home-equity loans. If this is your second time starting a company, perhaps you can borrow against your first, more established firm.

You will have to decide what level of debt makes you comfortable, and that depends on your personal circumstances and tolerance for risk. Do you have a backstop, like a large savings or even a wealthy family member who might be willing to lend you money? If you do, it might change your calculus.

Are you single? That can be both good and bad—good because no one else's livelihood will be impacted if your business fails, bad because there's no one but you to contribute to paying the bills.

A loan should be an investment that will pay off, not a move you make because you have bills to pay. "From early on," Ted says, "set yourself up to understand your margins. Understand how and if you're making money. Track your revenues and expenses, and match them as much as you can." A business owner might think she needs a loan, he says, when the actual problem is that the business's cash flows are not in sync. A loan won't fix that problem.

No matter what, don't overleverage yourself. Your cash flow should be four to five times your interest payments so that if the business fell by half or had a few bad months, you would still be able to make interest payments. Take the smallest loan you need and spare yourself both the financial and emotional stress of a loan you can't afford to repay.

SPECIALIST

In deciding how much you really need and devising a clear repayment strategy, SBA resources can be very helpful. "The SBA is the best-kept secret in the federal government," says Bill Briggs, who helped run the SBA's division that oversees loan programs. "There are many free resources out there, ones that you would otherwise pay a consultant to get."

For instance, the SBA can refer you to lenders and help you write a business plan, stand-alone or as part of your loan application, which can help you borrow the money you need. (For more on how to write a business plan, check out Chapter 2.)

SBA resources can also help you create a leaner business that needs less money to launch by matching you with coaches who can help refine any aspect of your business and connecting you with free or low-cost classes on a variety of business topics, including finance. These can offer perspective on how much money you really need, as well as how to spend that money for maximum impact.

With that information in hand, begin considering potential credit options.

Bill Briggs
Bill Briggs is former acting associate administrator, Office of Capital Access, a division of the Small Business Administration. Currently he works as a consultant in Arlington, VA. Running the 2020 Paycheck Protection Program is his proudest professional achievement.

Credit Cards

Credit cards get a bad rap, which can make sense. We all know people who've used their credit card too freely and gotten themselves into trouble. Plus, from a business perspective, credit cards can come with high interest rates—and paying off expensive debt while you try to get a business up and running can be overwhelming.

On the other hand, the debt you accrue through credit cards is flexible, with small minimum monthly payments and a balance that can go up and down as necessary. Credit cards aren't backed by assets and don't require a personal guarantee, so there is some flexibility if you aren't able to pay them off by a certain date.

Credit cards are also a quick way to get money, which could be important if you come upon an opportunity today that won't be there tomorrow. But as with any loan, don't get yourself in too deep. With credit cards, a mistake compounds very quickly.

Before you take any credit card, consider what's best for you, as there are many types of cards. Your business bank may be the easiest source of a card, as it may come with your business account. Alternatively, try shopping for a credit card and pick the program with the benefits you value. Some cards provide money back, and some provide free international currency translation. There is an infinite supply of options to consider.

Friends and Family

In day-to-day life, it can be easy to take money from family or friends casually, with no set expectations around repayment. In business, this is a mistake that can wreck relationships.

"If you take a loan from someone close to you, write down the terms so everyone knows what's going on," says Natalie Taylor. In other words, treat the loan as something more formal than simply an agreement between loved ones. You all should agree on when you'll pay back the loan, how quickly, and at what interest rate, as well as what happens if the business tanks or becomes a roaring success.

If it's a significant loan, discuss whether the lender will own any part of the business. The last thing you need is to accept $1,000 from your sister in the early days of your venture, only to find out she thinks she owns half the company when it takes off. Silent partners can sometimes get very noisy, so own the business by yourself if you can.

Agree on what will happen if life takes you by surprise. What if someone dies? What if a divorce or other emergency forces you to sell the business? Consider each possibility very carefully so you don't end up with a business partner you don't actually want to have.

Do not, under any circumstances, take a loan from friends or family if you're not confident that your relationship can survive a setback. If your business goes south, how will the holidays feel? Will you need to find a different set of godparents for your new baby?

If so, find a money source that comes with less emotional freight. About half of new businesses fail. They shouldn't take relationships down with them.

Banks

Bank loans are among the cheapest forms of debt, especially if you're able to get an SBA loan, since the SBA caps rates and fees.

If that appeals to you, go to sba.gov/lendermatch for a free online referral. Even if a bank doesn't work out, you may be able to get an SBA microloan from a nonprofit community lender, and many states also have their own microloan programs.

Bank loans are the least flexible kind of debt because they are typically for a fixed amount of money and repaid on a stated schedule. Moreover, banks typically look at historical performance in order to size a loan and decide whether to issue it in the first place. Thus, it's often a product that you use for growth capital rather than startup capital. Finally, there is also a business line of credit, which is typically a more flexible type of loan that floats with your need. It works like a credit card with a total limit, yet you also only pay interest for the amount of the line of credit that you use.

Fintechs and Online Lenders

On the internet, you can find all sorts of lenders that aren't traditional banks. Square, American Express, and PayPal are on this list, as are Intuit, Amazon, Shopify, QuickBooks, BlueVine, and NerdWallet, which bought the fintech Fundera. A Google search can help you find many more.

Some of these lenders require that you already have a relationship with their company—as a credit card processor, for example—before they'll lend to you. Others don't require any previous connection.

Either way, it can help to have a connection. Square, for instance, provides financing based on how much a firm processes through its point of sale system, then lets businesses repay loans at a pace that aligns with their revenue schedule. So if, for example, you're an ice cream shop,

Square might let you make bigger payments in the summer months, when business is booming, and smaller payments in the winter, when more ice is on the roads than in cones.

One of the benefits of online lenders is that they tend to say yes or no on loan applications quickly—often, according to Fundera founder Jared Hecht, they'll do so the same day you apply. By contrast, an SBA loan might take two to four weeks to process.

Of course, there's a trade-off: In all likelihood, you'll pay a higher interest rate over a shorter loan term with an online lender than you would with a bank. If you can profitably use the capital, however, that rate might be worth paying, especially if you need and can deploy the money into attractive projects that help you grow. Some online lenders make the service so easy that it's worth your time to get quick access to capital. Do your homework and check out your options!

Not every online lender is reputable. Some might deliberately lend a business too much money, then sue the business and lay claim to its assets when it doesn't repay the loan. Be sure to check out Better Business Bureau ratings and Google reviews. If it's not an online lender, then see where you can get references from other customers.

Also, ask potential lenders any questions you have—don't be shy! What rates should you expect? What loan duration? What percentage of the lender's business comes

SPECIALIST

Jared Hecht
Based in New York, NY, Jared Hecht started the online lending brokerage Fundera. He thinks the experience of making Paycheck Protection Program loans during the Covid-19 pandemic will make banks better at lending to small businesses.

from repeat customers? Are its rates better or worse than competitors—if so, why?

If you're working with brokers, you should also ask what kind of small businesses they tend to help. What lenders do they work with? How do they make money? Will their fee affect the cost of the loan? What product suite do they offer? How do they decide what lenders might suit you? Will they run a competitive process to find you a lender? If you don't get straight answers, hang up and look elsewhere. Don't forget to ask about their fees, too! You should think long and hard about paying a fee that could potentially be higher than the actual interest expense on the loan.

A Few More Tips for Securing a Loan

Before you apply for a loan, Ted Kosev says, you should be sure to check your credit and correct any mistakes you find.

You might be surprised at what you find when you look at your credit reports, like an unpaid doctor bill or a property lien you didn't even know you had. Call credit-reporting agencies and try to resolve the problem. They may give you the runaround at first. Persist. It's worth your time to clean up an inaccuracy.

Find out what kind of data a potential lender wants to see. A standard data package includes two years of tax returns, bank statements, brokerage statements, and a spreadsheet showing your net worth and cash flow. Prepare all of this data in advance so that you can easily send the files to multiple potential underwriters.

If your credit score is mediocre (approximately 550–660), be mindful of applying to multiple lenders who are making inquiries on your credit score. Multiple credit inquiries on your report can drop your score meaningfully, an impact you'll see for three to six months. If your credit score is above 700, you have more latitude to send your information to multiple lenders at once to find the best terms.

Ask whether a lender will make a soft inquiry or a hard inquiry on your credit. Hard inquiries (also known as "hard pulls" or "hard credit checks") generally occur when a lender makes a credit decision about a mortgage, loan, or credit card. You typically have to authorize these. The effect of a hard inquiry on your credit score ultimately depends on your overall credit health. In general, adding one or two hard inquiries to your credit report could lower your scores by a few points.

Adding a bunch of hard inquiries within a very short time, will likely have a greater effect on your credit score. This is because lenders see multiple credit applications in a short time as a sign of risk. Banks also see checking accounts as exposure, so opening a new one (at a different institution, presumably) could be a "hard inquiry" that affects your credit score.

Soft inquiries (also known as "soft pulls" or "soft credit checks") typically occur when someone checks your credit as part of a background check. This may happen, for example, when a credit card issuer checks your credit to see if you qualify for certain credit card offers. Your employer might also run a soft inquiry before hiring you. Unlike hard inquiries, soft inquiries won't affect your credit scores.

(They might not even be recorded in your credit reports, depending on the credit bureau.) Since soft inquiries aren't connected to a specific application for new credit, you see them only when you view your credit reports.

Bill Briggs suggests talking to three different lenders to see what you're offered and what feels right to you. Consider choosing a lender that can offer insights into your business. Some lenders specialize in particular industries, whether that's dentistry or restaurants, and they often know a lot about how to run a company in that space. Having an advisory relationship with a lender, in addition to a financial one, can be invaluable.

Your lender will have a lot of sensitive information about your business, so make sure you understand and believe in the quality of partner you are working with. In the worst and unlikely scenario, what happens if there's a security breach, especially if you store customer data? Ask if the lender has ever had a data breach and, if so, how they helped their customers in the fallout. It's a question that could safeguard not only your personal information, but your business as a whole.

Make Sure to Get Paid by Your Customers

While your bookkeeper is in charge of tracking your money as it goes in and out of your business, you're the one in charge of making sure customers pay their bills. Sometimes, it can feel like that's easier said than done.

Whether your business is consumer-facing or sells to other businesses, you'll need to decide how you'll accept payment. Cash, credit cards, apps, Apple Pay, Google Wallet, and bank transfers are all options. Use a variety of methods to make it easy for your customer to pay you. The easier it is, the fewer excuses they have to be late.

Many small business owners don't factor in the lag time between making a sale and getting paid. You'll need an invoicing system to audit what you expect to earn versus the amounts that actually come in. Some systems match invoices to incoming checks or bank transfers. Others match sales to a cash register, checking that the sales a register shows match the cash and credit slips in the till. There's no single system that works for every kind of business.

Decide on an amount of money that would matter to you if it weren't paid. That might be $200 if you're a smaller business, or $5,000 if you're a bigger one. Don't spend your entire weekend chasing sums under that amount. But if money is consistently going missing, you may have a bigger problem: a system error or theft within your workplace. Those kinds of discrepancies are worth hunting down.

Most important, adjust your workflow so that you get paid promptly. Even if you have good customers, if they are slow to pay you should consider adjusting your billing cycle. For example, if you are a trainer, you might have an automatic invoice system that bills after each appointment. That may be the easiest way to keep your clients up to date versus a monthly payment cycle. Spend the time to think about how to optimize this part of your business. Cash flow is a big deal!

Manage Payment and Performance Risk

Aylon Pesso
Together with his father, Aylon Pesso owns and runs Pesso's Ices & Ice Cream in Bayside, New York. His favorite ice cream flavor is roasted marshmallow.

At Pesso's Ices & Ice Cream, managing payment risk is simple. Customers hand over cash or a credit card—and if they don't, they go without a scoop. But if your business, for instance, produces $10,000 fans to cool nuclear reactors, you're going to need to find a better way to manage payment and performance risk.

What does that look like? Here are a few baseline suggestions.

Agreements and Documentation

Document the arrangements you make with customers and vendors. Verbal agreements are very difficult to enforce, so draw up a contract, even if it's simple and short, delineating the services you are providing, when you are obligated to deliver them, and how much you're charging. You can find templates online, or a lawyer can help you. Be very specific about what you're selling, how much it costs, and when you expect payment.

- Prove that the purchase reached its destination with tracking, a bill of lading, and a signed delivery receipt. Be sure to specify who owns products in transit.
- Deliver the goods in the way that the buyer specifies.
- Bill the correct party. It might not be the same party you delivered to.

- Agree on when customers will owe you the money after receiving the product. What event will trigger payment? Will they pay you when they receive the main product they're buying, or will they hold out until you send the maintenance manuals as well?
- Make sure your invoice includes the information the client needs. That might include the purchase order number, the invoice number, addresses, authorization numbers, or something else. Clients often have idiosyncratic invoicing requirements, and if you want to get paid, it's your responsibility to learn about and follow them.

Dealing with Payment Risk

"Every sale has payment risk: *Can* my customer pay? It also has performance risk: *Will* my customer pay?" says Karen Turnquist, owner of Sage Business Credit in Minnetonka, Minnesota. "Most of the time, when an invoice doesn't convert to cash, the problem isn't that the customer can't pay. The issue is that they won't pay.

"But mostly," she continues, "they're not trying to stiff you." The difficulty is usually that there's been a miscommunication between you and the customer about the sale itself. Karen suggests investigating the problem by reviewing the terms of the sale—was the sale clearly

Karen Turnquist
Karen Turnquist is CEO and founder of Sage Business Credit in Minnetonka, MN, which lends businesses money against their accounts receivable. Turnquist is a fan of clear, written communication. "If we have an agreement, we can write it down," she tells her clients.

described in writing?—and probing likely weak points when onboarding customers.

Here are some concrete steps to take to decrease payment risk:

- Pull a credit report from Dun & Bradstreet or Experian. You don't have to ask the business for permission. Dun & Bradstreet charges $189 for a single report and also sells packages of multiple reports. Experian also offers a subscription model that starts at $189. For sales in the tens of thousands of dollars—or more—it could very well be an investment worth making.
- Get vendor and bank references. Ask vendors about the terms of their relationship with your prospective clients, the average length of time that an invoice is outstanding, and whether they have been paid for their most recent sale. Is everything satisfactory? What's their credit limit for this company? You don't want to be a customer's single largest unsecured creditor. Ask the bank when the client's account was opened, its average account balance, and its average loan balance.
- Be mindful of how much "float" you are providing between the service and getting paid. Limit the amount any given customer can owe you. For example, maybe a customer buys $1,000 worth of goods from you every month; don't send a new order if that customer still owes you $1,500.

It's fine to choose different credit limits for different customers. You might require cash on delivery or partial payment in advance for a new customer or one who has been shaky about paying bills in the past—while providing longtime, trusted customers with a more liberal limit. Your goal is to strike a balance between making sure you're not at risk of being put out of business and also not overly inhibiting sales by being too cautious. Enter in a credit limit field on the page for each company in your records.

Update credit limits for your customers annually. A lot of businesses resist doing this. You shouldn't. According to Karen, "A real company will not have a problem with this request. You should not assume that a bigger company is more likely to pay, or that a client that has always paid always will continue to pay."

She adds that some business owners are less willing to ask for more information or set terms when a customer gets to be a very big part of their business. But that's actually when it's even *more* important to have current information and updated limits—because if your business is *dependent* on a single client, you want to make sure that client is *dependable*.

If customers are chronically delinquent, cut off their credit and don't lose sleep over it. "Three broken promises means you cut them off," Karen says. "The first time they're late, you call and make sure they have everything they need. After that, if they call and tell you that you'll have payment next week, and that doesn't happen, that's a broken promise. After three of those, you're done extending credit."

Every business wants to make sales; it's easy to forget that the payment is ultimately what matters. Don't succumb to the temptation to make sales at any cost. Hold out for customers who pay their bills and keep their word.

Staying disciplined is important in all parts of your business, but especially in finances. Staying attentive to your books and being assertive with your customers will keep your cash flow in the black, and you just might sleep a little better at night.

Questions to Consider

- What three banks will you explore as your business bank? Have you compared service levels and fees to make the right choice for your cash flow needs?

- Could you use an online bank or do you need in person service?

- How will you track profit and loss? What are the positives and negatives of using a bookkeeper in your business?

- How will you determine if and when you need a loan? How will you choose a lender?

- Where is the nearest SBA office? Have you looked for resources from government agencies that support small businesses?

- How will you make sure your customers actually pay their bills? How will you make sure the sales you make end with money in the bank?

CHAPTER 6

Brand Building and Marketing

For years before she opened her business in Manhattan, Courtney Foster had no special interest in hair. A conversation with celebrity hairstylist Ted Gibson changed that.

"He explained what made one of his haircuts different than the cut you could get in the neighborhood, and he encouraged me to go to school," Courtney says. "I didn't know there was a school to go to. I thought people just knew what they were doing."

As a single mother, Courtney had dropped out of high school to care for her infant son. As soon as she could, she enrolled in a GED program, which qualified her for cosmetology school. There, she did so well that the school asked her to come back and teach.

Courtney Foster has always been a hard worker with single-minded determination. In recent years, she has

Courtney Foster
Courtney Foster owns Courtney Foster Beauty in New York, NY. A conversation with Ted Gibson, who cut Angelina Jolie's hair, helped educate her about what makes a good haircut and inspired her to go to cosmetology school.

brought that all-in resolve to marketing her business, Courtney Foster Beauty. Every day, she uses social media to share information on her products, her services, and ideas to help clients do their hair at home between salon appointments.

"I think you should use all the social media platforms," Courtney says, though she likes Instagram best because it lets her post images of her process and finished styles.

She doesn't stop there. "On Facebook, I create hair-loss groups and plug in a lot of information and education," Courtney says. "I promote my book with healthy hair recipes and my hair-care products: a serum that helps with hair loss, stress-relief candles, shampoo, conditioner. I'm also working on two other books."

She is always asking herself one question: "What else can I create that's of service to my clients?"

Courtney Foster has figured out a fundamental truth about business: relationships are at the core of every successful transaction.

The Power of Relationships

Think about the person who cuts your hair. Unless you live in a small town or rural neighborhood, your area probably boasts more than one hairstylist or barber. If you live in a city, you might have dozens of choices within walking distance of your home.

Even if we ignore the stylists who aren't good at their jobs, you could still go to a different professional every month. If you're like most people, though, you consistently visit the same business, and the same stylist, over and over again. You might even keep seeing this person if she messed up her job once or twice, cutting your hair too short or leaving your bangs too long. (Believe us: we've been there, too.)

Why do you have that loyalty? Because you know your stylist. She knows you. After a while, you've been through life together, sharing what's happening at that new job or asking for advice about trying out some new highlights.

Even if you're selling something other than haircuts, that's the type of trust-based relationship you want with your customers. There will always be other restaurants, other mechanics, other jewelers. You want to form a bond with your customers, one that makes you *their* small business of choice.

Ali Cudby
Ali Cudby is a customer service expert based in Indianapolis, IN, and author of *Keep Your Customers.* She says that 70 percent of purchasing decisions are based on how a customer feels about the transaction.

"Seventy percent of purchasing decisions are based on how customers feel they're being treated in the transaction," says Ali Cudby, a customer service expert in with Alignment Growth Strategies in Indianapolis, Indiana, and the author of *Keep Your Customers.* "Feeling seen, heard, valued, and understood is vital for growth."

The Experience Matters

Joey Rault is a sales executive who helps business owners find ways to modernize their operation. As part of that work, he encourages them to think deeply about the experience they are providing. "Think about a Ben & Jerry's franchise," Rault says. "The primary experience is eating ice cream. But the owners also create an attractive environment in their store, with the goal of creating an engaging experience for the customer."

SPECIALIST

Joey Rault

Joey Rault is the head of sales at Orum, a fintech company building the technology for real-time payments. Joey's work focuses on creating a better, more transparent and efficient financial infrastructure for businesses to thrive. Joey lives in New York City with his wife, Courtney.

Lululemon, an athletic wear company, is home to yoga classes. Barnes & Noble bookstores have cafés; Equinox, the gym, offers coworking spaces. These extras are reasons to visit these shops rather than their competitors. They also bring people who aren't necessarily planning to make a purchase into the store, where they are an audience for desirable products. These places have attractive personalities that invite interaction.

Ikea does this, too, from the moment you walk into the store to the moment you leave. It starts with the furniture, which Ikea lays out in homelike rooms so you know how the chair you're considering buying would look next to a living room sofa. But Ikea isn't just helping your imagination along when it comes to choosing beds or coffee tables; the company is inviting you to picture yourself as the kind of person who has this beautiful living room—or whose children sleep in that adorable bedroom. To help you really reflect on the kind of home you want to build, they help you recharge with some signature Swedish meatballs and pastry when you get hungry exploring the store.

There are all sorts of ways for your business to create a signature experience. Wild Rumpus, a children's bookstore in Minneapolis, Minnesota, has cats and chickens hanging around the store at all times. Turn off the light in the bathroom and you'll see that there's an aquarium behind the mirror. There's also an area for exploration that can keep a child happily occupied for hours. Wild Rumpus sells books, but it's also selling a memorable experience, especially for kids. For parents, the Wild Rumpus customers with the real purchasing power, that's invaluable.

As you work to brand and market your business, it's that kind of personality that you should seek to create, expand, and publicize. It has to be authentic. No parent wants to arrive at Wild Rumpus only to discover that the staff members don't like animals or children who want to interact with their menagerie. Lululemon doesn't hire workers who hate yoga. Your business's personality needs to start from within, not just exist as a marketing conceit.

Market Through Your Customers

Once you've planned out the experience and relationship at the heart of your business, you'll want to get started telling others about what you offer. To begin, the best way to do that is through word of mouth.

"Word of mouth is the most powerful way to form a base from which you can grow," says Kathy Savitt, Yahoo!'s former top marketing executive and the current president and chief commercial officer at Boom Supersonic in Centennial, Colorado.

Eventually, your word of mouth will include people you've never met talking to each other. At the start, however, you need to introduce your company to a group of people who make up a logical first market for your product. Make sure to include people who already like you, feel a connection with you, and want you to succeed, like your college classmates or the parents of your children's friends. "Everyone has a following," Kathy says.

She also notes that most people who start businesses do so with the idea that they can be better than their competition in some way. Whatever good or service you're selling, you've probably found ways to make it stand out from the competition. Introduce your business to a core group of people who will appreciate those improvements.

Then, give your group a chance to sample your products. Maybe you'll provide them with free samples, a marketing expense that's much easier to afford if you're, say, making food than if you're making jackets from imported Italian leather. Either way, it might make sense to give

SPECIALIST

Kathy Savitt
Kathy Savitt is president and chief business officer. Kathy held senior positions at Yahoo! and Amazon and also was the founder of two start-ups.

your product out to friends and family with discounts—or maybe you'll ask them to pay the going rate, but you'll do so with an especially big smile.

Giving away products and services is one way to spread the word about your products and services. Another way to help boost word of mouth is through influencer marketing. There is a wide variety of influencers, ranging from micro- to macro-influencers. Micro-influencers are individuals with 10,000 to 50,000 followers who are known in one particular area like beauty, personal fitness, or restaurants. Macro-influencers have huge followings and usually large price tags that come along with their big fan base. Macro-influencers may not fit within your marketing budget criteria, but micro-influencers are more affordable. Pick someone who is known within your industry and also is a good fit for your personal brand image.

Next, you listen. Solicit reviews from these early customers and take their feedback seriously. Don't take the feedback personally. Do people want your product? What do they love about it? What don't they love? What more do they want from it? Their feedback can help you adjust your product, tweak your business plan, and even lead you to new opportunities. You need early customers who are passionate about what you're offering.

Our collaborator on this book, Ingrid Case, has a friend, Minneapolis-based Tim Klein, who left the corporate world and got a master's degree in health and wellness coaching. She hired him for six months of weekly nutrition counseling sessions. Now 15 pounds lighter and much more aware of how much sugar she can eat before she feels

Ingrid Case
Ingrid Case is a writer, journalist, copywriter, editor, and co-owner of INCase LLC.

lousy, Ingrid can't stop talking about how great Tim and his services are, and she's sent several new clients Tim's way. That's what a happy early customer can do for your business.

As your business grows, you'll follow the same pattern, Kathy Savitt says: always expanding to a new group of customers, then listening to the feedback. "Invent, listen, optimize," she says. "That becomes a flywheel you can build your entire marketing effort around."

Know Your Audience

Listening to that initial feedback is crucial. When you know for sure what your product is and who your customers are, you can begin to invest in other ways for people to find you, such as social media posts, a blog, or advertisements in local publications or broadcasts. If the core business proposition isn't right, though, these subsequent efforts can be misguided and expensive. It's important to know what matters most to your audience so you're communicating in a way that will resonate.

"I have a friend who was going to do monthly gift boxes," Kathy says. She expected that her customers would be parents sending care packages to college students. Instead, her boxes were a hit with adult children sending care packages to parents in assisted living. "She should have figured out her audience before she bought packaging, put a website together, designed a logo, and all the rest of it," Savitt says.

Knowing your audience and what needs or challenges your products and services solve for your customers both ensures that you have a fit between your product and the market and guides your marketing efforts. It empowers you to share a value proposition that your audience will respond to.

Consider Marketing Partnerships

Sometimes it's hard to build word of mouth among people you already know, because the communities you're a part of aren't actually your target audience. If, for instance, you've invented a toy, and your network includes neither kids nor parents, you will need to look elsewhere to generate buzz.

In that case, consider a marketing partnership. "There are other small businesses out there that see themselves as serving the same audience," Kathy says. A store that sells clothing for children, for instance, might love to host your toys as a limited-time offering. Their customers—folks who are already shopping for children—are much more likely to give you the feedback you need.

In addition to customer feedback, pay attention to referrals, amounts purchased, and frequency of purchases. "When you start seeing repeat customers, you have a viable business. Then you can start to pour more gasoline," Kathy says.

In marketing, that gasoline could take the form of a website, emails, advertisements, social media posts, or loyalty programs that reward your most frequent and valuable customers. These can lead to a cycle of repeat business that propels business growth.

Design Your Website

With a sense of your business's personality in place and your early influencers on board, you'll want to expand your target audience beyond customers who know you personally. That's where your website and social media come in.

Whether you plan to sell goods and services online or not, you need to have a web page. Most prospective customers will take to Google to check out who you are, what you're about, and if you're legitimate before they even consider buying what you're offering. A website should present information about your business—its name, logo, location, and hours, in addition to anything else you think would be informative, like photos—in a way that reflects your business's personality.

Your website is also a place to tell your story. Why are you in business? What's your business all about? At Callie's Hot Little Biscuits in Charleston, South Carolina, the owner made sure her website noted that the recipes for her biscuits came from her grandmother. That kind of detail helps you introduce yourself and invites customers to connect with you on a human level.

Andy Montgomery, lead designer at Square, says that business owners should think about website design earlier than you might imagine. "From the very beginning, start setting aside funds for investing in design" he says. "Some kind of foundational brand design is table stakes for starting out."

Hire a designer to create a logo, a color palette, and a typeface, Andy says. If money is tight, start with just a logo. Plan a budget of $500 to $2,000—enough to design a brand identity that can stay in place for years.

If your website will have a lot of text, you may also want standard layout templates, which you can find online. Think about the tone you want for your site; it should stay consistent, both on your website and in your emails. After all, you can convey a lot about your business through the way you write. Depending on your target audience, you might choose to be informal and funny, heartfelt, technical, or more formal. Your communication style should match your business's personality.

We understand that an initial investment in your brand standards might feel like you're splurging on an expensive haircut from an expert stylist. But with the initial investment in place, you can maintain this image in the same way

SPECIALIST

Andy Montgomery
For over 20 years Andy Montgomery has led design efforts for companies of all sizes, from small businesses to the Fortune 500, along with building his own digital agency. He's passionate about bringing together a deep focus on craft and quality with brand and product experiences that create an emotional connection.

a less expensive stylist can follow the expert's lines every time you need a trim.

There are also several tools that enable business owners to create their own website without the use of a designer. These sites offer design templates and include step-by-step instructions for setting up your business's site. Service providers include Squarespace, Wix, Shopify, WooCommerce, GoDaddy, and WordPress.

Use Search Engine Optimization

You've spent time, energy, and money to build a terrific website, so of course you want potential customers to find it. This is where search engine optimization comes into play. Most consumers discover products, brands, and services by searching for them online. You want your business to surface in search queries on the first few pages. To do this, you'll need to use the same keywords in your website copy that people searching for a business type into a search engine, such as Google.

How do you know what words potential customers are using when they search online for businesses like yours? Sebastien Edgar, a search engine optimization expert in San Francisco, says that you should do three things.

First, go online and search for "free keyword research tool." That third-party tool will tell you what words a person who wants to buy what you're selling types into a search engine. Maybe you sell cupcakes. A keyword research tool might tell you that people who want to buy cupcakes often search for "dessert," "bakery," "cupcakes," and "gluten free."

Second, get a free account with Google Search Console. This tool can tell you about the actual searches that have led people to your website. Let's say you sell running shoes. Google Search Console can tell you that the people who have clicked on your website have been searching for "running shoes," "running," "local running events," or "tennis shoes."

Third, align the results with your copy. If people who want tennis rackets are ending up on your running shoes page, that's a misalignment. Adjust your copy and keywords so Google will show your website to people who are looking for what you're selling.

SPECIALIST

Sebastien Edgar
Sebastien Edgar has over 10 years of SEO experience, and he has helped Fortune 500 companies and brands optimize their web presence. He loves digging into analytics data and is hands-on to interpret and shape the story it tells.

Hire a Photographer or Take Your Own Pictures

Try to avoid using stock photography as much as you can, because it looks generic and customers sniff that out easily. If you can afford it, hire someone to take pictures of your products and process. It's worth the expense. "You can get one photo shoot done and use those photos for two years," Andy says.

A photo shoot isn't in the cards for small business owners just getting started. This isn't a problem since you can always take your own photos. If that's best for your business, getting some cheap or free advice from a professional can help.

Aundre Larrow, a photographer and art director based in Brooklyn, New York, says that your photos should reflect your value proposition. For example, if you run a neighborhood pie shop that uses all-natural ingredients and prides itself on a kind, cozy atmosphere, then your photos should look homey and natural, not slick. That tone and brand personality should inform your choices of what you photograph and how you frame the image. You also need to think about your website's color palette and how the photographs you select fit into that palette. All of these elements create your brand's personality, look, and feel.

SPECIALIST

Aundre Larrow
Aundre Larrow is an expert in photography, art direction, creative and social strategy, community managing, copywriting, and photo research.

You can take good photos with your phone, Aundre says, and when you do, he suggests that you use lighting on your subjects to make them pop—or take a picture somewhere with natural light. Put simply, don't photograph your pie in the basement. People should be able to see your product, and the image should look inviting.

The two to three hours after sunrise and before sunset tend to offer the best lighting, and overcast days can be ideal. Photos taken outdoors in the middle of a sunny day often have odd shadows, but the middle of the day can be a great time to use indirect light—through a long row of windows, for example.

Separate yourself from your subject and then your subject from its background, with the subject perhaps three to five feet from you and the background another two feet behind the subject. "This allows you to create depth," Aundre says, noting he also likes to play with color. Use color to make your subject pop. You can employ a single accent color or use color theory to help. Many small businesses sell food, which they need to photograph for menus, Instagram, and websites. To photograph food well, Aundre says, get a bounce card: a big, matte white board, such as Styrofoam, poster board, or white cardboard. Place the bounce card on the opposite side of the food item from your light source, where the object makes its shadow. If you want even more light, you can add another white surface underneath the object to form a corner.

For food photos, also consider colors and sizes of other items, such as plates or napkins. "Use smaller plates than you think," Aundre advises. "If the plate is too big, it takes over the image. Make the food proportional to the plate size." Take pictures from every side of a product, he says, and play with the images.

Hairstylists, he adds, should show pictures of a service in process or of customers looking great after a cut. "Don't take pictures of people in your chair unless you are working on their hair," Aundre says; it doesn't make for a flattering shot.

Plumbers, mechanics, and other tradespeople should use photographs to illustrate how to do something, like changing a tire or bleeding a radiator. Showing photos of employees who will visit clients' homes or businesses can also build trust.

"A matte white bounce card or additional light source can also improve photographs of people with darker skin tones. Consider using an additional light above the subject, so you can see the person's hair in the photo," Aundre says. "Be a partner to people who don't look like you. Ask, 'Do you feel good about this image?'"

Above all, Aundre says, "Take a lot of photos. Capture the natural joy of your business. Customers should look happy to be there."

Communicate with Email and SMS

When people make a purchase from your company, ask them if you can contact them in the future. Collecting email addresses and phone numbers from customers can be a valuable marketing tool—because, unlike on Google, where customers need to actively try to reach you, email allows you to reach them. Plus, customers who give you their contact information are usually interested in what you're selling and therefore likely to buy again.

Customers are quick to click the unsubscribe button, though, so send emails and text messages strategically and don't overdo it. Make sure that you're emailing about subjects that are important and immediately relevant to your customers. No one wants to feel pestered, so knowing what your audience wants to hear about is especially critical. Customers like to hear about sales or if there is a change in your operating hours, but they probably don't want to hear from you twice a day.

Courtney Foster, for instance, regularly emails the customers of her beauty business about new products and services—but she makes sure they're things her customers might genuinely want to buy. During the Covid-19 pandemic, for instance, customers got weekly updates that included tips and tricks on doing their own hair. Her young adult son served as a model for video haircare demonstrations.

"People feel like I still care, that I didn't forget about them," Courtney says. The response has been good, and she plans to keep the momentum going.

SMS or text message alerts are also a helpful way to alert your customers to promotions or remind them of appointments or reservation times. Service providers like Twilio, TextMagic, Simple Texting, Salesmsg, or EZ Texting have products that enable business owners to connect with their customers.

Connect with Social Media

Done well, social media is a way to promote your business while connecting directly with potential customers. Rather than acting as a one-way channel for you to send out information, it allows you to receive feedback, too, and respond to it—all in the time it takes to type a tweet or a Facebook comment.

Many business owners see social media as intimidating, but it doesn't have to be. Begin by figuring out where your audience already is, suggests Nick Dimichino, social

Nick Dimichino
Nick Dimichino
is a family man,
wannabe chef, and
aging hockey player
from New Jersey.
When he's not
daydreaming about
opening a sandwich
shop in Italy, he's
a brand marketer
focused on social
media content and
creative storytelling.

media lead at Tidal. You should have a presence, even if it's a small one, on Instagram, Facebook, and Twitter. "Have a good, easily findable website, and use your Instagram account to push viewers to that website," Nick says.

Pick a platform where you'll concentrate most of your efforts. For most retailers and food businesses, Instagram is the logical choice, since you can show off pictures of your products. Facebook is a good pick as a secondary platform for a retailer or food business, or as a primary channel for a mechanic, animal hospital, dry cleaner, or other kind of business that isn't primarily visual. Instagram is a more visual platform; Facebook contains more text-based content and links back to other websites. You want your business's social content to fit the platform you're using to communicate. Writers, editors, and other professionals whose work shows up in print and online often use Twitter to push out links. If you make videos as part of your work, TikTok might be a good use of your time.

New inventory, weekly specials, promotions, and other news—put it all on social media. You can generally get away with communicating more frequently on these platforms than you do via email. There's no hard-and-fast rule regarding the number of updates you should post. The correct frequency depends on your business and what's happening with it—and the type of response you're getting on each post.

"Three to five posts a week is a healthy dose of communication," Nick says. Create a routine. Perhaps on Monday you post about your products. On Wednesday, you post about an employee, and Friday's post is about a community connection.

As you go through your workday, keep your need for social media content in mind. If you are launching a sale, a daily special, or a buy-one-get-one deal, post that. Your customers will want to know about it. Behind-the-scenes content is also often a hit, especially if your business does something customers can't do—or, at least, can't do as well as you. Showing off how you make ice cream or how you shoe horses, for instance, could give your business a unique face.

Tell your founder's story, too. Talk about your schooling and training, what led you here, your passion for the work you do. Explain why you choose particular materials. You want people to share these posts. Each time they do, they're endorsing your content, so make your posts as interesting and engaging as you can.

It's easy to fall behind on your posts and feel that only your mother likes or shares them. It takes time, consistency, and patience to grow a social media presence. Figure out a way to fit it into your daily routine. If help is available from someone who is excited about this part of your business, consider accepting it, especially if you're not fluent with social media or don't enjoy it. You might have a cashier who would love to make social media part of her job—with your approval before posts go up, of course.

Fortunately, there are several good self-serve marketing platforms that businesses can leverage to spread the word about their business and services. These include, but are not limited to, the following. Some of these services include both free and paid opportunities:

- **Facebook and Instagram.** You can create a Facebook or Instagram business page for free that is used to share content, information, stories and promotions. While the page setup is free, if you want to promote your content you may have to pay to get more eyeballs. Both Facebook and Instagram offer a variety of tools that help businesses advertise directly to their customers. These tools are designed to be easy and intuitive, so you don't need to hire a marketing expert to use them.

- **Google and YouTube.** Customers discover businesses by searching on Google and YouTube. Fortunately, Google has a great self-serve platform that allows business owners to create free business profiles (website, contact information, and hours of operation) and manage and create search and video ads. They also offer a plethora of training courses, including free certification in digital marketing so you can learn how to optimize your Google ads.

- **TikTok.** Within TikTok there are also a variety of tools to help business owners connect with their audience. Businesses use TikTok to share more stories about their business, and TikTok helps by providing video templates and tutorials. Additionally, like Facebook and Instagram, TikTok offers a self-serve platform for buying ads. TikTok can help match your business with influencers and content creators through its Creator Marketplace.

- **Twitter, Pinterest and Snapchat.** These are three additional platforms that have resources for business owners to connect with their customers, serve ads, and measure results. They offer self-serve templates to help businesses create ads that are endemic to the platform.

With so many choices, it's good to pick one or two platforms initially. You should pick the platform based on where your customers are spending time. Since consumption patterns differ by platform, there isn't a one-size-fits-all approach that can be used across all of these platforms. Be patient. It can take time to optimize your marketing on these channels. Remember to test, learn, and iterate.

Consider Traditional Advertising

More traditional kinds of marketing—print advertising, radio spots, and television ads—are also worth considering.

Alana White, executive media director for Giant Spoon, a marketing agency based in New York and Los Angeles, says that you should consider where your customers are, then design marketing to reach them there. If your ideal customer reads the *New York Times*, a print or online ad there could be a good investment. If your business sells fried clams to beachgoers, a billboard near the beach or a banner pulled behind a plane could find your audience in a very targeted way.

SPECIALIST

Alana White

Alana White is the executive media director for Giant Spoon, a new kind of marketing agency designed for the future of communication, built from the ground up.

This kind of marketing can be much more expensive than social media. Alana says that radio is probably the lowest-price option, and a good thing to consider after maximizing your digital channels. Print advertising is the next option, followed by television and billboards as the most expensive.

Don't forget the possibilities in showing up to community events and sponsoring local activities, Alana says. Having your name on the local Little League team's shirts can garner a surprising amount of exposure.

Take Advantage of Earned Media

There's another way to get good publicity in local publications or broadcasts. It's usually referred to as earned media—and it's free. The process is simple: just reach out to reporters or editors with press releases or even cold calls to let them know about something that's going on in your business: an event, an interesting sale, even a new employee with an interesting backstory.

Sponsoring community activities is also a way to get free press coverage. If your business is opening, if you're offering a new service, or if something else new is going on, reach out to local media and see if they are interested in sharing your story.

Just like your customers, reporters are also interested in your company's backstory and human element. If your business is reaching an important milestone like an anniversary, use that moment to get media attention. These are all ways to reach new customers without spending a dime.

Consider boosting your paid advertising or offering your customers a promotion during the same time period. This combination of free and paid media offers the greatest return on your investment, because the two forms boost each other.

That's true for everything we've discussed in this chapter: all of these marketing strategies build on one another. If you're posting about a sale on social media, make sure you ask your customers to tell their friends about it. If you have an article written about you, post it on social media. Sometimes, it might take a while to generate marketing momentum, but when you start to create some buzz—and you will—make sure to maximize it.

Questions to Consider

- What do you know about your customers? Who are they? What do they love about your business? What can you offer your core customers to show them that you value and appreciate them?

- Who are the customers you don't have today whom you need to grow your business? What do you know about them?

- How will you reach potential customers? What avenues haven't you considered—online and off?

- When you're communicating with new or existing customers, what's in it for them?

CHAPTER 7

Hiring and HR

Like most restaurant owners, Marc Bash is always looking for good help. Between the four restaurants he owns with his brother, he has employed upwards of 250 people over the years. Cooks. Waitstaff. Bookkeepers. You name it. That's because, like most restaurants, Marc sees a lot of turnover.

Every year, among the 15 million people who work in the American restaurant industry, 70 percent change jobs. So, if you're running a restaurant, you're always hiring. In the process, you learn quickly what works—and what doesn't.

Some restaurants use ads and job boards to find potential workers, but Marc believes strongly in a principle he's developed through a number of

Marc Bash
Marc Bash and his brother, Jon, own restaurants in New York, NY, a lineup that has included a pizzeria in Union Square, an Italian restaurant called Frittelli, and Cafe Luka.

successful—and less successful—hires over the years: good employees attract good employees. "If I like someone, I ask about that person's siblings, cousins, and friends," he says.

Many eateries see previous restaurant experience as a prerequisite for new hires. Not Marc. "I want to know about a potential hire's personality. Does he or she like people? I like happy-go-lucky people. I don't want you bringing your bad days to work."

Marc also wants people who are willing to do tasks the way he wants them done, and people with previous experience sometimes aren't willing to do that. For instance, he once hired a cook who strongly believed in putting just one kind of wine in Bolognese sauce—but Marc prefers to use both a cabernet and a merlot. The cook also didn't think pine nuts belonged in pesto, which Marc sees as heretical. The two butted heads at nearly every turn, and eventually the cook walked out.

"I'd rather have someone who is raw and really wants to learn," Marc says. "I expect to train people in the way I like to do things, and they need to be willing to do things my way."

Marc's hiring techniques might not be perfect for everyone, but they've helped him find people who fit well and stick around. "If I like you, you can rise through the chain: start as a dishwasher, then a busboy, then a waiter, then a cook or a manager," he says. He walks the walk, too: one of his managers started as a busboy who didn't speak English, and now, two decades later, he's Marc's right-hand man.

Even if many of his employees don't stay for long, most of Marc's hires have worked out well, he says, and he's had to fire surprisingly few of them. "If I've had 250 employees over the years, I've maybe fired eight of them."

In the end, Marc says, it's simple: "I'm good to the employees, and they're good to us."

Depending on your business, you might want to take a different approach to hiring than Marc does. If, for instance, you work in an industry that requires specialized skills, it might be a bad idea to bring someone onto your team with no prior experience. But regardless of what your company does, figuring out a hiring process that brings in quality employees and works with your style will be among your most important tasks.

Because, when push comes to shove, a business is only as healthy, only as strong, and only as valuable as the people who work for it.

Embracing Your Role as a Leader

Starting and running a business isn't easy. It's a huge lift. Doing it well will affect every part of your life. You'll taste joy and success, and you'll also have times when the challenges seem insurmountable. Occasionally these opposites will occur on the same day. You may feel that you're simply making it up as you go along, doing the best you can on the fly.

Being deliberate about the approach you take to leading your company, however, can be a very worthwhile place to spend some effort. Your leadership style will profoundly affect your company's success, the experience your employees and customers have with your business, and your personal and professional well-being.

Take Responsibility for Your Role

Ron Beller, a CEO coach in Aspen, Colorado, says that every company founder creates and models the organization's culture. "People are looking to you to see how to behave," he says, "so be intentional about the kind of behavior you are modeling."

Mistakes happen in any human endeavor, so consider how you will respond to your own and other people's mistakes in your business. It's better, Ron says, to consider errors as an opportunity to learn, rather than creating a culture in which it's usual to blame other people when things go wrong. "If a mistake happens, put all your energy into fixing the problem and moving forward—not into deciding who to criticize. What happens next? What will we do differently?"

Too many people are more interested in being right, and in affirming their rightness, than they are committed to learning. Because a boss has power, eventually employees of such a boss will learn that they are rewarded for confirming what the leader already thinks. That stifles the flow of real information in an organization—and information is a business's blood supply.

Don't be the kind of boss who can't tolerate hearing news that's less than ideal. Commit to curiosity, conversation,

SPECIALIST

Ron Beller

Ron Beller is a CEO coach in Aspen, CO, and previously was a partner at Goldman Sachs.

and questions, encouraging the open (yet polite!) exchange of information across your enterprise, even if what you hear doesn't support your own vision of what should be.

Build a culture of clear communication. When you agree to do something, be very specific about what you will do and when you will do it. Let people know when you can't do something so you can negotiate. "People mostly live with sloppy agreements," Ron says, because they're afraid of the conflict that may ensue if they tell another person, "No, I can't do that." Model a culture in which "no" is the beginning of a negotiation, not the end of the world.

There will be lots of things about your business that you can't control. Focus your energy on what you can control. Hiring is within your control. Use that to surround yourself with people you are excited to have on your team. Give them context and autonomy.

Take your time on reference checks. References will often shout about someone's good qualities and whisper the negatives. There are no perfect employees, because there are no perfect people. Even so, slow down and find out more about the strengths and weaknesses of the candidate in front of you.

Among college admissions counselors, it's axiomatic that there is no best college—there's the college that's the best fit for a given student. The same is true of employees. Think about how employees' strengths can complement one another while also offsetting each other's weaknesses. "Create roles where people spend 80 percent of their time on what they love doing," Ron suggests. If someone isn't thriving in a role, consider whether there is another job in your organization that would be a better fit before severing the relationship.

What Are You Doing for Yourself?

Your business needs your attention. Before that, however, you need your own attention. Looking after your own well-being is key to surviving and thriving as a business leader. It's also an important component of succeeding in business. When you take good care of yourself, you are a more effective leader. You also come up with better, more original ideas.

In any business, "so much comes down to how leaders are looking after themselves," says Megan Jones Bell, clinical director of consumer and mental health at Google. She was formerly chief strategy and science officer at Headspace. "There's a clear spillover impact."

SPECIALIST

Megan Jones Bell
Megan Jones Bell is clinical director of consumer and mental health at Google. She was formerly chief strategy and science officer at Headspace. She spends much of her time thinking about issues of mindfulness, mental health, and work-life balance.

Megan says she sees business owners under a lot of daily stress. Pushed and pulled by competing demands, they often find it difficult to exercise, eat well, and practice other good-health basics. "All that stuff can be hard to implement, especially for people who are responsible for other folks," she says.

A solution, she says, involves training yourself to live in the present moment. "Be aware of what you're feeling and thinking, but without engaging with the emotional charge," Megan says. Mindfulness, she continues, is a combination of awareness and acceptance of how things are right now. When you bring present-moment awareness to more moments, you get a greater capacity to stay calm and focused. That benefits you and other people in your orbit, both at work and at home.

Take purposeful breaks, Megan suggests. Create routines and rituals that support your transition from work to home, like ten minutes of uninterrupted meditation or an extra five minutes spent driving a more scenic route. "Routine should be enjoyable, something that interrupts the pattern of rushing between things."

When you take a break at work, choose a pause that brings you in better connection with yourself or someone else. Touch base with a friend. Meditate or move; stretching and walking are both good choices.

Go to a different room if you can't go outside. If you eat, choose a snack that's nutrient dense.

When you're less stressed, you're more credible, empathetic, and trustworthy, as well as less reactive and irritable. You're less likely to take the bait in aggravating situations. You help create a culture where other people also feel free to look after themselves. The overall result is a less stressed, more collaborative working atmosphere.

Taking Care of Yourself Can Also Create Customer Insights

Learning about your own pain points and need for mindful care can also offer insight into customer experiences, says Lisa Kaye Solomon, a writer and educator at Stanford University's Institute for Design.

SPECIALIST

Lisa Kaye Solomon
Lisa Kaye Solomon
is a writer, educator,
and advisor who
teaches at Stanford
University's Institute
for Design in
Stanford, CA. She
believes that people
can grow and change
through effort and
deliberate practice.

"You need to understand your customers' days," Lisa says. "What's their experience? Where are the pain points? Where are the points of emotion? How can you deliver delight and/or alleviate pain points?"

Like Ron, Lisa points to the importance of open communication. Most people fear that, if they say something unpopular, they'll be made to feel stupid and wrong. "We learn faster in environments where people can speak openly," she says. "Cultivate an experimental mindset."

Looking for opportunities to grow is important as well, even if that growth is bit by bit. "Do you believe that you can grow and change through effort and deliberate practice? Or is there a fixed mindset where you are either smart or not smart?" Lisa asks. If you don't believe that you can grow, do you believe it's possible for other people?

Like Megan, Lisa advocates for going slowly and living in the present moment. "Our formal educations are geared toward getting right answers, fast. There is no reward for the daydreamer, the divergent questioner. It's no wonder that when we get to the real world, we hustle to get to the answer," she says.

In business, however, rushing can mean that we don't understand the question well enough to devise really good solutions. "I always tell students at the beginning of classes that they will only fail if they come to me in the first hour with a solution to a problem," Lisa says. At that early point, they understand the problem too superficially to invent a lasting, innovative solution.

Emphasize mindful, thoughtful growth in your own company culture, and you'll expand the chances that your business will have better, longer-lasting ideas.

Scaling Your Team

If you're running a restaurant, like Marc Bash at the beginning of this chapter, you'll have to hire help right away, and keep hiring as people come and go. With other kinds of business, however, you will be the company's only employee in the beginning. That's a healthy starting point and one that will teach you a lot about yourself, the business you want to run, and the basic value proposition of the entire venture.

Doing everything yourself also lets you learn every role in your company, from high-level strategy to bookkeeping. When you do everything yourself, you understand where the money comes from, as well as where it goes. You're forced to understand your business completely, and that means you'll know what you're looking for in each potential hire. You'll also know exactly how you want the pieces to fit together. For instance, if you clean your own vacation rental properties, you'll have a much better sense of how long it takes to do the job than if you never spent time mopping the floors.

As you become more familiar with all the systems and roles within your business, you might find yourself overworked—or overwhelmed. That means the day has come when you need to hire help.

How quickly you reach that point depends on your individual circumstances: the kind of business you're running, the skill sets it requires, and how fast it's growing. If you're not good at or don't enjoy a certain part of the business, it makes sense to move someone else into that role as soon as you realistically can. Likewise, if you do particularly enjoy a certain role, that's probably not the first candidate for outsourcing.

You could be a solo accountant for years, for example, but as more and more clients come your way, you'll have to either turn down work or hire help. You might be able to run a food truck on your own, but you almost certainly can't run a full-service restaurant by yourself.

When you're scaling up, be strategic about how you spend your time. You may love some tasks, but be careful that you don't hang onto a job out of enjoyment or habit when letting someone else handle it would free you up to do more strategic work. You will know the business better than anyone else, and your time is best spent putting that unique knowledge to use as efficiently as possible.

Making that first hire isn't always easy. You may find it difficult to trust someone you've only recently met with important pieces of the company that is your livelihood. If you're running tight margins, it can be hard to convince yourself to spend money on a hire that may not pay off immediately. Thriftiness is a good quality, but it shouldn't come at the cost of your mental health or your ability to manage your business's growth.

When Is the Right Time to Hire?

Heidi Schriefer, head of human resources at Grindr, an LGBTQ social networking app, has a simple formula for when your business needs to hire. "When you can make more money if you hire more people and can clear the cost of them on payroll, that's when you hire more people," she says. "If you're constrained by lack of manpower, then you increase the manpower."

Let's go a little deeper. You'll know that you're ready to hire when doing so addresses one or more of these issues:

- You can't run the business by yourself.
- You're turning down work.
- You've identified potential new revenue sources, but you don't have the bandwidth to pursue them.
- The quality of what you're selling is suffering.
- You don't have time to do your daily financials, bookkeeping, and other paperwork.
- You need someone with a specific skill set that you lack.
- You can't take a break or a vacation.
- Your company isn't growing.
- Customers can't reach you.

Heidi Schriefer

Heidi Schriefer is vice president for people and places at Grindr in Santa Cruz, CA. She says there's a simple way to decide how much time to give a decision-making process. "The amount of time you spend making a decision should be directly proportional to the irreversibility of that decision."

- You can afford the hire.
- Hiring gives you a meaningful time refund, meaning you can focus yourself on pressing matters within the business.

These aren't hard-and-fast rules. There could be times, for instance, when you can afford to make a hire, but it feels like more trouble than it's worth. In general, bringing people onto your team can go a long way toward making your company operate more effectively. Ultimately, you will have to listen to your gut.

Get Help at Home, Too

When you're thinking about hiring for your business, you should also think about whether having an extra hand could help you take personal tasks off your plate and allow you to focus more on your job. Childcare and home tasks need to get done, but don't think you need to do everything yourself.

Our collaborator, Ingrid, and her husband, a cartographer, spent at least two hours a day, sometimes more, driving their son to and from school. They loved the time with their child, but after a while, they realized they couldn't miss that much work, so they hired his longtime babysitter to do the driving for them. The babysitter and their son enjoyed the time together, and the arrangement let the parents be more productive during the workday. As a result, when their son got home from school, they could be more attentive to him.

Ingrid's family also regularly prepares enchiladas, which are delicious but time-consuming to make, because they require a tomatillo-based sauce. They typically make the sauce in August and freeze enough to last through the year. This year, they didn't make the sauce themselves. They hired a friend to do the job and applied the time refund to work. While these examples might seem trivial, they highlight how important it is to find options to maximize your time.

A housecleaner, a wash-and-fold service at the local laundromat, and grocery delivery can all save you time—and as a small business owner, time is your most valuable resource.

Good Help Is Hard to Find

Good employees can be the difference between your business thriving and your business failing. You'll trust your employees with something that's vitally important to you, and you'll probably spend more waking hours together than you'll spend with your family.

Yet businesses often make hiring decisions based on a résumé, some recommendations, and a short conversation or two. That's not enough. Thinking strategically about your hiring process can greatly improve your odds of finding the right people.

Here are some questions you should reflect on before starting your hiring process:

SPECIALIST

Aaron Zamost
Aaron Zamost has
led communications,
policy, and people
teams at a wide
range of technology
companies including
Square, Google,
and YouTube.

What Is the Job?

Before you begin the hiring process, get clear about what your new teammate will do. "Lots of CEOs aren't willing to let go of anything, so they hire people who will do their bidding," Aaron Zamost says. "Start by identifying the things that only you can do." Then begin the process of outsourcing other roles to a potential new worker.

Start by writing a job description. The clearer you are about your expectations, the more likely someone is to do the job well. By the same token, if you're confused or uncertain about what you want from a worker, no new hire will be able to make you happy, no matter how amazing that person might be. Feel free to use job descriptions from the internet as a starting point, but be sure to customize them to your particular situation. No job is too big or small for clarity, and having a description from the outset also becomes a way to measure results and manage expectations.

Freelance or Employee?

Payroll can easily become the biggest expense for a small company, especially when you hire full-time help. That's why many businesses bring on freelancers instead of employees—because doing so can help you save money and help you determine what kind of help you do and don't need. Because freelance roles are typically hourly or project-based, they let you experiment with what's working and what isn't. Is having a bookkeeper as helpful as you thought it would be? Does having a bartender improve your bottom line?

Not every job can be handled on a freelance basis. Employment law sometimes requires businesses to treat someone as an employee. The distinction may be more technical than practical in many cases. In others, having freelancers may provide flexibility to make changes in the relationship more easily. If you want to learn more about the classification of these roles, the IRS offers detailed information on how to make that determination at www.irs.gov.

In a nutshell, the law considers three categories of information when deciding whether an employment relationship classifies a worker as an employee or an independent contractor:

- **Behavioral:** Does the business control how the worker does her job or behaves while she's doing it?
- **Financial:** Does the business control financial aspects of the worker's job? Is the employer in charge of deciding how the worker is paid, reimbursing expenses, and buying tools and supplies?
- **Relationship features:** Does the worker get benefits? Is the relationship ongoing and open-ended? Is the worker expected to work only for this business while she has a job to do there? Is her work a key part of the business?

If the answers to the questions above are yes, it's likely that you're looking to add employees. The more control you expect to have over workers' behavior and your mutual financial arrangement, the more likely it is that you will need to bring them on payroll. A barista will need training, a work shift, maybe a uniform, and supplies arranged and paid for by your company. She'll do things the way you tell her to do them. If she's full-time, you might expect that she won't work for another coffee shop while she's also working for you. This person is probably an employee.

The person who creates your website, on the other hand, does the work on her own computer system, wearing whatever she chooses, using skills that you didn't teach her, during whatever hours suit her. You both understand that she has other clients. This designer is a classic freelancer.

Using freelancers in a targeted way can help you get specific tasks accomplished without building up your ongoing payroll.

Using freelancers can also let you bat above your average. Maybe you couldn't afford a world-class web developer as a full-time hire, but you can afford to pay for her services on a project basis. It's never been easier to find and hire tremendously qualified people for a wide variety of projects.

A hybrid option also exists: a contract-to-hire arrangement. Ask someone you're considering as a full-time hire to complete a project for you as a freelancer. Pay market rate and treat the project as an audition. You get a sense of this person's abilities and working style. She gets a sense of what it's like to work for you.

Create a written agreement detailing the terms of the project: what the person will do for you, by when, for how much. (Online sites such as Rocketlawyer.com can help you create a contract that meets legal requirements.) Be sure to include an end date on the arrangement so that you can revisit if the relationship works for both of you and whether you might benefit from a more full-time option.

You might also consider part-time workers. A part-timer can help you cover a particular time slot or function that you need regularly, but not daily. Think of a pharmacist who always works Sunday hours to offer the pharmacy owner a day off. A part-time worker probably isn't the best choice if you want someone to devote all her mental energy to your business, but it's often a useful short-term solution. It can work well, though, if you are able to find specialized talent with unique needs.

If your business has a busy season and a slow season, you may also need seasonal employees, like camp counselors or gift wrappers who provide a helping hand when you're jammed. For these scenarios, focus on the types of people who might be best for these roles and channel your efforts into a more niche recruiting strategy. Not everyone wants a full-time job, and many have unique flexibility around time off where they may want to earn extra dollars or stay engaged. Take advantage of these opportunities and think broadly about workforce options.

Where to Find Freelancers

Word of mouth is often the best way to find independent contractors, so ask around in your network and industry. After all, as Marc explained, there is no better endorsement for a worker than a recommendation from someone you trust.

If that fails, there are also web platforms that can serve as good hunting grounds, like Upwork, Fiverr, and Indeed. They let you hire a company or an individual and allow you to search at a wide set of price points. An additional benefit is that these platforms expand your pool of potential workers. For something like web development, you aren't constrained by geography in terms of who you hire.

How to Find Employees

Finding good employees is perhaps the hardest thing a business does. That's at least partially because many business owners aren't good at defining what they want from an employee. To address this problem, you should ask yourself a few questions:

Aylon Pesso
Together with his father, Aylon Pesso owns and runs Pesso's Ices & Ice Cream in Bayside, New York. His favorite ice cream flavor is roasted marshmallow.

What does success look like for someone in this job? Imagine that you're at your employee's first annual review. What qualities and accomplishments will make you excited and happy?

Think carefully about the words you're using and how they foreshadow the groups of people who will likely respond to them. Aylon Pesso of Pesso's Ices & Ice Cream in Bayside, New York, puts job requirements on their website. Among other things, they're looking for workers who are at least 18 years old and willing to work at least all of June and July, plus most of August. The employees need to be able to lift and carry 30 pounds up and down stairs, bend and reach into freezers, and scoop frozen desserts. The business doesn't specifically ask for college students, but by the nature of the description, that's who responds to that listing.

How much experience do you want in a hire? It's important to ask yourself what skills a person will already have, and what skills you will want them to learn once they start working for you. "This is a classic missed step," Aaron Zamost says, referring to the expectation that candidates will already have the skills they need to do the job.

Consider the difference between demonstrated professional experience and capabilities that are more intrinsic. Parents might be world-class multitaskers, but it might not show up on their résumé. Do you need someone with a long career history in a particular job, or do you need the skills they possess, like ability to multitask or strong organizational skills?

The same goes for educational credentials. If you advertise for someone with a PhD, be very clear about how that PhD will help you. If what you really want is someone who is smart, creative, and loves to learn, the PhD might not be necessary.

Will you hire people for a role that's at their level, below, or above them? If a role has an opportunity for growth, you might consider hiring someone you think is overqualified for the current position. Or, if you think the job is teachable and the applicant's other qualifications are a good fit, you might be more willing to hire someone who's underqualified on paper. If you choose to do that, though, do so with the understanding that this hire probably won't be very good at the job for a while. It'll take time to coach him up. Don't get frustrated. Instead, make a plan to slowly phase him into the work, rather than putting a lot of responsibility on him from the get-go. That way, you can set the employee up for success—and keep your expectations in line.

Are you married to your physical location, or could you hire someone to work for you from a different location? Plenty of excellent business relationships can thrive, even if the parties never see each other in person, especially if the arrangement is freelance. The Covid-19 pandemic proved how many industries could adapt to a culture of remote work with the benefit of modern technology. Keep your eyes open for remote arrangements, even if you haven't used them before.

Where will you search for job candidates? The places you look for applicants depend on what kind of business you have, and there's no wrong way to go about it. The best advice is usually to cast a wide net—the more applicants you have, the more likely you are to make a great hire.

As with freelancers, word of mouth can be an effective way to find employees. LinkedIn can help you find a variety of professionals, too. Reach people whose jobs are visual on Instagram, and consider advertising in niche professional publications to reach candidates for other jobs. Recruiters and public relations companies can also spread the word about your company and your search.

The Job Interview

You don't need to know the details of every potential employee's five-year life plan. You do need to clearly explain the job you need done and ask questions about the person's ability to do that work. Get specific. What will success in this role look like? What metrics will this person need to meet? Write down the points you want to make and the questions you'll ask in advance of the interview.

If you're like many small businesses making an early hire, your needs may be relatively simple. You want someone who is reliable, honest, cheerful, and able to do the work. Pesso's Ices & Ice Cream doesn't need to see résumés, and Marc Bash might be happy to give a young person his first job as a dishwasher. If that's your circumstance, you might just need to clearly explain the job and ensure that the applicant can do it and do it well.

You can also explore applicants' background and abilities with more depth. One way to do that is to take a detailed look at people's résumés with an eye toward talking with applicants about what mistakes they've made and how they've grown from those experiences.

Try to find out how well regarded a person was at her various jobs by asking, "What would your boss say about you?" or "What would your coworkers say about you?" Better yet, follow that up by asking for references, so you can see how the two sets of answers align.

Consider whether people have been promoted within their company. If they've changed employers every year or two, that can be a sign that they didn't gain the trust of their organization. Ask questions about moving around or gaps, though neither is necessarily problematic. A candidate might have moved from one company to another because her boss moved and took her along. A résumé might have a gap because someone had a baby or needed to handle a health issue.

Grindr's Heidi Schriefer says there are several questions that she usually asks. They include:

- What differentiates the good from the great in what you do today? "The level of response someone gives me tells me whether they look at their job in a narrow way or a broad way," Heidi says. You want a broad thinker, someone who understands how their role affects multiple parts of the business.
- Tell me about your best day at work. What made it great? "I don't want someone to tell me about their easiest day at work," Heidi says. "Good stories need conflict and hardship. Show me how you overcame challenges."
- Why did you join your current company? Why have you stayed and what would make you leave?

Taken together, the answers to these three questions can help you learn what motivates someone.

If your business already employs a team, you could ask multiple people to join the interview process. For some roles, you'll want to check out hard skills, soft skills, cultural fit, and management expertise. You could also talk through a case study with an applicant as a way of seeing how this person thinks and solves problems. Getting a variety of opinions about the candidate can give you a fuller picture and a wider variety of insights. It can also help with team cohesion, because a bigger portion of your workforce will have been included in the decision-making process.

Diversity, Equity, and Inclusion

You might be your company's only employee, potentially for quite a while. When you begin hiring, though, it's smart practice to build a diverse workplace.

"It's not only the right thing to do, but also the best business decision," says Alicia Burt, an executive working in diversity, equity, and inclusion at the San Francisco, California–based nonprofit All Raise, which works to advance gender equity in tech. "The more diversity you have in your team, the better you do financially and the more creative you are."

A 2019 McKinsey study considered companies that were in the bottom and top quartiles, first for gender diversity, then for ethnic diversity. The companies with the highest gender diversity were 25 percent more likely to have above-average profitability than those with the lowest gender diversity. For ethnic diversity, the difference was 36 percent.

Building a diverse workplace isn't as simple as hiring some women and people of color and calling it a day, Alicia

SPECIALIST

Alicia Burt
Alicia Burt works in diversity, equity, and inclusion at the San Francisco, CA–based nonprofit All Raise, which works to advance gender equity in tech.

says. To get started, you'll want to be explicit about your values as a leader. A commitment to diversity and inclusion has to start at the top. "Articulating that can create a shared understanding and atmosphere," she adds.

Look at the workplace you have now. Do existing employees feel that they have equal opportunities to succeed?

Whether you already have a workforce or are just beginning to hire, think about what will make all employees feel respected and that they belong. Recognize other cultures' holidays. Make your bathrooms gender neutral. Choose inclusive images for your marketing material. Show cultural sensitivity all year long, not just during Black History Month or Pride Month. "I've seen employers make the mistake of focusing on hiring before they ensure that they have an inclusive workplace and culture," Alicia warns. "That makes for a lot of retention problems."

Once you're confident that your workplace culture values and supports all your employees, regardless of background, prioritize recruiting talent from diverse backgrounds. Interview a diverse slate of candidates for every open role. Examine your job postings and make sure you're stating your desire to build a diverse workplace.

"Actively source candidates from diverse communities," Alicia suggests. "Work with local organizations and newspapers. Explore the possibility of hiring customers by putting up job ads in your workplace."

Make sure you have the workplace supports new hires may need. For example, if you hire new mothers, have lactation space. If you hire Muslims, give them time and space to pray, plus a place to wash before they pray.

After you've hired a diverse group of people, work to keep them by creating mentorship opportunities and continuing to build a supportive environment where they can grow their career. "Turnover is expensive, plus it signals to other underrepresented people that not all people can succeed at your company," Alicia says.

Focus Not Just on Your Bottom Line, but on Your Culture, Too

The people you hire need to be able to do their jobs—so if you need a software engineer, don't go out and hire someone who doesn't know how to code. But while it's *necessary* for an employee to have the skills required to perform, it's not *sufficient*. Employees also need to be a good fit for your company's culture. If they are, they will work seamlessly with teammates—and they will be happier themselves.

Company culture is less about what your company does than how it feels. What are your guiding principles? How do you work together? How do you treat one another? Your culture sets the business's unspoken norms and helps employees operate without needing specific rules for everything. It can even be a factor that attracts potential employees or like-minded customers—as is the case with mission-driven companies like Patagonia and Ben & Jerry's.

No matter how large or small your business is, take the time to think about your values. Your business will evolve a culture, whether you like it or not, because that's how human social groups work. You might as well take the time to intentionally seed an environment that's in keeping with your vision for the company. What values will move the needle in your business? Do you want to be the trusted local resource? Or are you the national expert? Do you expect people to be available 24-7, or are off-hours off limits?

A well-considered company culture moves the needle externally and internally, so employees can stand behind a vision. Many employees are attracted to purpose-driven businesses. Recreational Equipment, Inc., better known as REI, is a good example. Here's its statement of purpose:

> At Recreational Equipment, Inc. (REI) we believe a life outdoors is a life well-lived.
>
> We believe that it's in the wild, untamed, and natural places that we find our best selves, so our purpose is to awaken a lifelong love of the outdoors, for all.
>
> Since 1938, we have been your local outdoor co-op, working to help you experience the transformational power of nature. We bring you top-quality gear and apparel, expert advice, rental equipment, inspiring stories of life outside and outdoor experiences to enjoy alone or share with your friends and family. And because we have no shareholders, with every purchase you make with REI, you are choosing to steward the outdoors, support sustainable business and help the fight for life outside.
>
> So whether you're new to the outdoors or a seasoned pro, we hope you'll join us.

Read that and you'll have a good sense of who should work at REI. What's your business's purpose? How does it inform your hiring decisions and attract the people who should work there?

It's almost inevitable that elements of your personality will be reflected in your business culture. Maybe you like to email rather than text—you might see that reflected in how your business operates day-to-day. Maybe you're from a diverse background, so you value multicultural input and inclusion. If you have a family member with a developmental disability, you might start a business that's like Ada's Café in Palo Alto, California, which is named after the Americans with Disabilities Act (ADA). It hires only people with disabilities and has a culture that celebrates what people can do, not what they can't.

Or look at the fishmonger shop at Seattle's Pike Place Market. The people who work there aren't just fishmongers. They're also entertainers, throwing and catching fish and joking with customers. Fun and teamwork are strong parts of that company's culture, internally as well as to potential customers.

Sometimes a cultural value might mean that workers have to accept something that makes them uncomfortable at first. At Bubbly Paws, a pet-grooming business in Minnesota's Twin Cities, groomers have video cameras in their individual room workspaces. Miller says that the filming offers protection to both dogs and their groomers. To gain

Keith Miller
Keith and Patrycia Miller own Bubbly Paws Dog Wash in Minneapolis, MN. Keith sometimes brings his employees cupcakes.

acceptance of this practice, he approached each groomer in person, explaining what he was doing and emphasizing that only the company's owners would have access to the footage. He began with the easygoing employees and worked toward those who might be more anxious about the change, inviting people to talk with him about any concerns.

If a value doesn't personally resonate with you, it probably doesn't belong in your initial sketch of a desirable company culture. That's because cultural values must be authentic to succeed. Don't tell the world that you're transparent and then make all of your employees sign strict nondisclosure agreements. If you don't believe in your firm's cultural values, employees and customers won't, either.

Should You Offer Benefits?

As an employer, you'll have to decide whether or not you'll offer your employees health insurance, paid vacation, paid sick leave, retirement plans, or a suite of other possible perks.

As of January 2021, approximately half of Americans get their health insurance as a benefit from their employers. Offering health coverage as a benefit makes you a much more desirable employer. If you don't offer it, it's going to be harder to attract top talent.

Full-time staff members at Pampered Pooch Playground and Bubbly Paws get health insurance, with the business paying 60 percent of the premiums. Workers typically pay $25 or $30 for a doctor's appointment. "If you're sick, I want you to go to the doctor," Keith says. Keith also offers groomers cushion pads to stand on and encourages employees to use clippers more than scissors, since scissors can cause repetitive motion injuries.

You'll have to choose between many possible healthcare programs, each with different deductibles and coverage schemes for everything from hospital visits to prescription costs. Make sure you think not just about your own needs, but your entire workforce. To find the plan that's right for you, ask questions of both the healthcare plan representatives and your employees—while, of course, respecting their privacy.

You should also consider the messages you're sending with the benefits your company offers. Who actually uses them? Are they skewed toward the old or the young, women or men, parents or nonparents? Think about what your workforce would value. If you're a restaurant in Big Sky, Montana, it may make sense to offer ski passes as a benefit, but that same benefit won't have the same value in Houston, Texas.

After healthcare, the second-most important benefit to consider is paid vacation time. Everyone needs time to recharge, and if your employees don't have days off, they may start getting burned out.

Sometimes the law makes benefits decisions for you. Your company is federally required to provide Social Security and Medicare contributions, unemployment insurance, and workers' compensation coverage. If you have more than 50 full-time employees, you're also required to provide health insurance and family and medical leave. Under the Family and Medical Leave Act—FMLA— workers are entitled to up to 12 weeks of job-protected, unpaid leave every year for qualifying family and medical reasons, such as having a baby or caring for a dying parent. Additionally, a federal law requires offering 26 weeks of the same unpaid, job-protected leave for caregivers of military service members. Depending on where you're located and the size of your company, local and state laws may have additional requirements.

Your company's employees will get federally mandated holidays. Beyond that, though, you'll get to choose what holidays your business observes. What observances resonate with your business culture? Think about religious holidays, too, as well as religious practices during the workday. If you have Christian, Jewish, and Muslim employees, you probably shouldn't give workers time off for Christmas while making them use vacation days for Yom Kippur or Eid al-Fitr. Think about who your workers are and put together policies that are considerate of their needs.

In the end, the decisions you make regarding trade-offs like these will help your employees self-select. "A small company can't be all things to all people," Heidi says. "Will the attraction be that you'll train them, pay them more, offer better benefits, or be super flexible? Excel in an area and hire people who care about that."

Managing Payroll: Automate or Outsource It

Creativity on the public-facing side of a business gets all the glory, but there's a lot of possible creativity in the back office, too. Handle back-office functions well, and you can save time with automated functions such as payroll. Moreover, back-office automation enables you to have more analytical tools at your fingertips from software.

Unless you have specific business reasons for handling your back-office functions in-house, plan to automate and outsource everything you can. If you insist on doing it yourself, pay careful attention to how many hours you're devoting to tasks like bookkeeping. (For more on hiring a bookkeeper, see Chapter 5.)

Business owners who try to do their own onboarding and payroll tend to spend far too much time and energy accomplishing something that might cost $30 a month to outsource. Homebase, the payroll automation app, surveyed users, asking how much time they spent managing schedules, tracking time, and running payroll. The average: five to six hours per week. Don't underestimate how many other things you could accomplish with that amount of time on your hands.

An HR automation solution, such as those available through Gusto or Intuit, will help you comply with federal and local labor laws. For hourly workers, software lets you automate payroll processing from end to end. It's like automatic bill pay, but for your firm's employees. The Homebase app lets workers clock in and out and manage scheduling. Gusto is a good solution for salaried workers, because it includes a template offer letter and onboarding process. You may also need a system for keeping track of freelancers, for whom you will have to fill out a 1099 tax form if you pay them more than $600 in a calendar year.

Using technology to help manage people can help you reduce the kind of errors that can lead to employee frustrations and a lot of additional work. This is important: when you're a business owner, it's on you to fix your mistakes and pay for any damage those mistakes cause. Settling a wage or hour lawsuit isn't cheap; on average, it costs between $7,000 and $20,000.

Retaining Talent

Employment might be the only human relationship that begins with the expectation that someone will eventually walk out the door. All the same, you want to keep good employees for as long as the relationship is productive. Build an environment that offers as much freedom as possible, while still retaining loyalty. Get rid of toxic people quickly, before they can sour other employees. Not liking their manager is a leading reason employees give for changing jobs—so if there's a manager in your ranks who drives employees to the exits, it may be worth considering removing that person.

It's also important to identify employees who show promise and help them to grow as workers. Learning is important in every business, so giving employees mentoring and education will strengthen not just their skills, but their loyalty as well. Train your team and give them new opportunities, whether that means letting them work on a special project, offering to send them to a conference or enroll them in an online class, or giving them the chance to lead an internal process at the company. Give workers a few hours to learn from someone else or take a class in person. Sometimes, it could even be fun—and informative—to let your employees temporarily trade jobs with one another to better understand each other's pain points.

Many small business owners skip performance reviews, especially when they just have a couple of employees. Don't skip these. Regular reviews keep expectations aligned and everyone focused on a common goal.

One way to handle review meetings is to talk about what a worker is doing well, where this person has opportunities for growth, and ways in which the individual went above and beyond, making contributions that are outside her usual responsibilities. If your company has specific metrics for particular jobs—billable hours, number of calls taken in an hour, and so forth—those should also be part of a review.

Annual reviews are well and good, but they're not nearly frequent enough, Heidi says. "People need to know three things on a regular basis: what are my priorities, what am I doing well, and what could I be doing better? You'll never have to write a performance review if people know those things," she says.

Instead, Heidi has regular one-on-one meetings with the people who work for her. Some of those meetings are status updates. Sometimes they're about knowing the person better or responding to a crisis. And sometimes they're geared toward growth and development, which is where review conversations take place.

At Pampered Pooch and Bubbly Paws, every six months, Keith Miller surveys employee happiness. Workers answer five or six questions online, revealing how happy they are, what the business could do better, and whether they would recommend the company to a friend. This could be done confidentially if you think employees are reluctant to share tough feedback associated with their name, or it could be asked openly.

The owners aren't looking for praise, Keith says, but for opportunities to improve. He remembers an employee who once graded the entire company as a 2 out of 5 because they weren't recycling. "That was an easy fix," he says. "We just hadn't thought about it, and she was passionate about the environment. We put her in charge of recycling." Another person wanted a quiet place to go for five minutes of regular downtime. That, too, was an easy request to accommodate—and it's an improvement Bubbly Paws was only able to make because the owners solicited information from their employees.

Keith also tries to find ways to show appreciation to his workforce. When groomers volunteered to design buttons for Twin Cities Pride, for instance, he donated supplies, sold buttons at the front desk, and donated the proceeds to Pride.

Firing Employees

Even with the best hiring and management strategies, you'll sometimes make a bad hire. The situation doesn't have to be disastrous to be the wrong fit. Some people just aren't getting the job done. Some are toxic for your work culture. Others are benign presences but don't offer much productivity. You want a group of employees who are really contributing, people with a deep desire to be excellent at their jobs.

If you suspect that someone lacks what he needs to perform at a high level, there's a good chance that you're right. Anyone can have an off day, so don't rush to any judgments. But if you begin to feel concern, watch closely for two weeks. Pay attention. Don't tell the employee that you have doubts. Instead, focus on whether this really is the right person in the right role.

Maybe the problem was just a blip. But if not, there's no use in delaying your decision, because procrastination won't improve the worker's performance or make it any easier to have a tough conversation. Leaving the wrong person in place for too long can do a lot of damage to your company, and it's not fair to the employee, either. There's probably another company out there where this person will thrive. Once you are confident in your decision, sever ties as soon as you reasonably can.

"Ask yourself if you would hire this person again if you had that chance," Heidi advises. "If there's any hesitation, you need to dig in further."

Heidi also suggests looking not just at what the employee contributes, but also ways in which the employee causes problems. "Look at gross contributions versus net contributions," she says. "A lot of times managers get stuck because someone is a good gross deliverer. But what about the ways that you have to clean up after them? Are they energy givers or takers?" If someone's net contribution is a lot lower than their gross contribution, that relationship may deserve a closer examination.

When Keith Miller has to fire someone, he tries to make sure that it isn't a surprise. At Pampered Pooch Playground and Bubbly Paws, employees get regular feedback and chances to improve. He also makes sure that he and the employee have a witness for that difficult conversation. "I fire people with someone else there, because you never know what someone is going to claim," he says. "I won't just stand in the back room with someone."

When you end a relationship, do it from a place of gratitude for the good parts of your relationship. Be calm, clear, and kind. If you can afford it, give your fired employee severance pay. That won't make firing people any more pleasant, but it will help you sleep at night—and help them get by while they look for a new job.

In the end, you want a place where all of your employees want to do good work each day. That means hiring the right team, incentivizing their work with proper pay and benefits and, when needed, moving on from someone who doesn't quite fit.

Questions to Consider

- Do you want employees? If so, when—and what purpose would they serve?

- Where will you use freelancers? Full-timers? Part-timers?

- What culture do you want in your business? What values matter to you? Do your employees know and understand your values?

- What benefits will help you retain your team? Who do your benefits favor?

- How will you track your workers' performance? What kind of reviews will you use?

- When a relationship isn't working out, how will you end it?

SELF-MADE
BOSSES

Letitia Hanke

Sarah Korpela

Peter Stein

Andrew Hypes

Jen Pratt

Ilana Wilensky

Min Park

Germanee G

Courtney Foster

CHAPTER 8

Roadblocks

When Letitia Hanke launched her roofing company, she signed her contracts, "L. R. Hanke," for two reasons:

She didn't want customers to know she was a woman.

And she didn't want them to know she was Black.

Prejudice wasn't new to Letitia; she had been teased and ostracized for her race from childhood. At age eight, it got so bad that a teacher taught Letitia to play the trumpet during lunch so she wouldn't have to spend recess with her bullies. But when you're a business owner, Letitia came to realize, discrimination becomes more than an affront to your dignity; it is also an existential crisis for your bottom line.

This became clear to her early in her career when, as the owner of ARS Roofing, Gutters and Solar, she made a sale over the telephone to a couple who

Letitia Hanke
Letitia Hanke owns ARS Roofing, Gutters and Solar in Santa Rosa, CA. Her first job was answering phones at a roofing company.

157

were enthusiastic about having their home reroofed. She dressed in business attire that a stylist had chosen for her and went to the couple's Santa Rosa, California, home to get the contract signed.

The couple had been warm over the phone, but at their home, they gave Hanke a glacial reception. "I rang the bell, and when the wife answered the door, I introduced myself and put out my hand," Hanke says. "She reluctantly shook it. When her husband came over, he looked at my hand, and then at me, and then at my hand, and then he walked away." The wife came into the room, looked at her, and said that they'd had second thoughts. They were going to hold off on reroofing their home for now.

"I said that was fine," Hanke recalls, "and I turned to go. As I was walking out, the man came back and told me that they had an alarm system, and that it would go off very loudly if anyone tried to break into the house.

"I got into my car, drove around the corner, parked the car, and bawled my eyes out."

◆　◆　◆

Depending on who you are, you might never face the kind of challenges that Letitia has had to confront, but no matter what you look like or where you are from, every business faces challenges.

Even if you could plan perfectly and execute that plan exactly—things no human can do—your business is only partly under your control. Big and little problems can and will crop up. Some of them will be new, products of an ever-changing marketplace and ever-evolving world, as so many entrepreneurs witnessed firsthand during the Covid-19 pandemic. Others will be part of your business from the beginning, and circumstances will just make them more or less apparent.

Common issues businesses confront include unexpected expenses, unreliable employees, changing consumer behaviors, world events, demographic changes, traffic interruptions, new competition, and discrimination.

No one likes business disruptions. On the other hand, the same tools that can help you spot and survive bumps in the road are also good tools for managing your business generally. Don't lament your bad luck. Control what you can control. Dealing with obstacles and crises can teach you important lessons about yourself, your customers, and your company.

In this chapter, we'll help you roll with the unexpected. Doing so successfully usually includes two steps:

First, be observant. Analyze your company's data. Review your sales information. Watch for trends and talk to customers. Sometimes a big change—like the Covid-19 pandemic—sneaks up on you in a few weeks. More often, though, changes take place gradually over months and years. No one announces them or holds a press conference. The world stays mostly right side up.

So, try to read the trends. Notice them and adapt accordingly, before a shift grows into a crisis for your business.

Second, be flexible. There is more than one way to run your business. Regularly ask yourself questions about what you

Sarah Korpela
Sarah Korpela owns Luxury Estate Managers of Aspen in Aspen, CO. Her clients, she says, are able to treat their homes like five-star hotels: one call gets them whatever they need.

could do differently—and then evolve. Remember: Like Letitia, you may not need or want every client that comes your way.

Sarah Korpela, president of Luxury Estate Managers of Aspen in Aspen, Colorado, agrees that flexibility, imagination, and ability to pivot are the keys to success. "It's not the survival of the fittest. It's the survival of the most adaptable," she says.

Here are a few examples of how self-made bosses adapted in the face of change—particularly in a once-in-a-generation pandemic that no one could have expected but that forced everyone to adjust.

Find a New Group of Customers

In February 2020, Peter Stein had a robust business selling Little Peconic Bay oysters to restaurants all over New York. One month later, in March 2020, the pandemic shut down New York. "Our restaurant business ended on a dime," Peter says. "No one was traveling or going out to dinner."

Peter could have panicked or quit or done things the way they'd always been done. Instead, he retooled his business to sell directly to consumers. He used his network of friends, family, and business contacts to spread the word that he would deliver oysters directly to customers' doors. A cousin who had written software to optimize school bus routes helped him create efficient delivery schedules.

"I sent out a survey asking people whether they would consider buying oysters like this, and every survey came back as an order," Peter says. "The business grew and spread out geographically. I made between 1,500 and 2,000 deliveries in the first month. There was one week where I matched my income from before the pandemic, but it nearly killed me. I was working 12, 16, 18 hours a day." The burden of childcare for his young daughter fell entirely on his wife, making it a taxing time for the whole family.

Peter Stein
Peter Stein owns Peeko Oysters, which is on Long Island near New Suffolk, NY. He can't remember a time when he didn't love oysters.

A friend told National Public Radio about his business pivot, and soon the prime-time radio show *All Things Considered* ran a feature about Peter. "The floodgates opened," he says. "I was recruiting people to help me deliver and keep up with orders. Because the show was national, I got a fan call from a guy in Dallas, Texas. At one delivery, a passerby said, 'Hey, are you the guy from NPR?' and bought oysters from me on the spot."

One of Peter's buddies in Brooklyn polled his friends, and together, they ordered $1,200 worth of oysters. When Peter delivered the order to their building, neighbors came down with the customers and bought yet more oysters.

By the winter of 2020, Peter had pivoted again, this time to shipping retail orders via UPS. Because more people stayed on Long Island after Labor Day than in years past, he was also able to make deliveries closer to home.

Sell an Adjacent Product

Etsy, the online marketplace for handmade and vintage goods, sold basically no masks in March 2020—except for Halloween costumes. But, in April, with the pandemic clearly underway, the company sent out an all-points bulletin to its sellers: make masks. They were right. Within months, mask makers had sold $500 million worth of a product for which there had previously been zero demand.

Like Etsy, you can learn to read your market. Is an issue long term or short term? How can your company adapt to the situation?

Andrew Hypes
Andrew Hypes is a DJ and producer based in Richmond, VA. He began playing the drums in the third grade.

Andrew Hypes, a DJ and music producer based in Richmond, Virginia, is another example of someone who successfully began selling a product adjacent to what had been his core offering. When clubs closed in March 2020, Andrew's work disappeared, because the kinds of parties where DJs played were no longer safe. Much of his production work also ground to a halt. Andrew didn't give up. He realized that most of his engagement came through Instagram, so he used that channel to advertise his availability to teach music and music production lessons online.

"That's what I did for the first three to four months of the pandemic," he says. "Then things started opening up, so I dropped the teaching back a bit. I've been swamped with projects, but I could go back to teaching if I needed to."

Let Go of What Isn't Working for You

In Sandpoint, Idaho, Jen Pratt built Fresh Sunshine Flowers in part on her willingness to deliver flowers to just about anywhere in the area. But after three years in the business, Jen found herself stressed and constantly ill with whatever bug was going around. So she made some big changes, including letting go of daily flower deliveries. "I was spending so much time stressing and driving around, and it wasn't profitable enough," she says.

Jen Pratt
Jen Pratt owns Fresh Sunshine Flowers in Sandpoint, ID. She began her business by selling out of a box truck with a side window, back when food trucks were at their peak.

Instead, Jen is focusing on things that are special, meaningful, and profitable, a list that includes weddings, her floral subscription service, and arrangements to sell through a local grocery store. "The grocery store option lets me say, 'I can't deliver, but if you need flowers in a hurry, here they are,'" she says. Together, her choices give her consistency: a chance to plan how much she'll work and how much she'll earn in any given month.

"Sometimes I have a feeling of guilt, plus a fear of missing out, but I know I do my best work when I'm not exhausted," Jen says. "I could have started saying no about six months earlier, and I wouldn't have been as stressed. It took me getting really sick in a stress-related way to start saying no."

Diversify Your Products and Geography

Quick diversification can help your business weather a storm, and making sure that you're always diversifying as part of your standard business practice can also help you get through the inevitable shake-ups.

In March 2020, no one expected that many Americans would work from home for more than a year. Companies were thrown into a new work model, and many realized their employees didn't all need to live in the same place—and neither did their customers.

Ilana Wilensky
Ilana Wilensky is president of Jewel Branding and Licensing in Atlanta, GA. Her agency represents designers and brands to license their trademarks and designs to manufacturers across a wide range of consumer products that are sold through retail channels.

A shift to online sales, either instead of or in addition to a physical location, requires an easily navigable website, good security that keeps customer information safe, and product ratings and reviews. Once you've figured all of that out, making the transition can be a game changer for your bottom line, as long as you consider what delivery options make the most sense for your market and business.

Diversifying your business offerings can make you more resilient, too. Ilana Wilensky is president of Jewel Branding and Licensing in Atlanta, Georgia, where her work involves collaborating with artists and designers to help them get into the consumer products game. About two years ago, Jewel started a creative services division, which works on product design and development for clients. The move helped diversify the company, making it less reliant on any one income stream.

Having a variety of products has also helped Jewel stay afloat. "During the pandemic, people weren't shopping as much for clothes and handbags," Ilana says. "But home products did very well." The same diversification can help the company thrive through other market changes, long after the Covid-19 pandemic is history.

Geographical diversification has also helped Min Park, a restaurant consultant and investor, keep the lights on at Omakase Capital, which works with restaurants in Northern California. The company likes scalable concepts, he says, which is why one of his restaurants, Rooster & Rice, has nine locations, while another, Bamboo Asia, has four.

"If you're a restaurant with multiple locations, you have a much higher chance of being in business in 20 years than if you have one location," Min believes. "The reason is psychological. A bad meal is a very negative experience. When peo-

Min Park
Min Park is an ex-finance professional (JPMorgan) who invests in hospitality concepts such as Rooster & Rice and Itria, technology, real estate, and cryptocurrency.

ple figure out what they want to eat, they don't like taking risks. They gravitate to consistency." If you're offering food they know they like, you have an advantage. If you're close to home for your customers, that's even better.

When people are stressed and tired, Min says, they're even more likely to choose known, trusted brands—because they are in no mood to take even a small chance that dinner won't be delicious. If they order takeout, the same risk aversion applies. This time it's because customers know that takeout food may not be quite as delicious as the same meal eaten at the restaurant, so they pick a place with food so excellent they know it will still be good by the time it arrives.

Sell What Your Customers Are Buying

A former merchandiser at The Gap, Germanee G styles high-profile women for their professional and personal lives. Before the pandemic, her clients almost always attended meetings and events in person. By the end of February 2020, she says, all her clients were canceling. "After award season, the pandemic put our company in the dark for almost four months; we were convinced it would end our business completely," Germanee says. "I thought the business would be over."

Germanee G
Bicoastal wardrobe stylist, Germanee G provides branding solutions and wardrobe styling to some of the fiercest thought leaders, game changers, and trailblazers making waves in startups and Fortune 500 corporations.

As the year unfolded, however, Germanee realized that her clients still cared about looking good, and many of them had virtual public appearances to make. "Our business resurfaced after the unfortunate death of George Floyd, since many of our clients are women of color who hold C-suite positions," Germanee says. "They had to show up and look the part on company Zoom calls, social platforms, and media outlets and support their businesses and communities through a heart-wrenchingly difficult time."

Clients hired her to style those appearances. Before long, she realized her business could be adapted to a new paradigm.

Other clients were enjoying wearing more relaxed clothes, but still wanted to look pulled together and professional on screen. Companies have hired Germanee to give talks about how to show up as your best self, and she offers a virtual class on the same subject. "I thought we would be lights out, but it's been very much lights on," she says. "I've learned to be nimble, stay connected, and branch out into new opportunities to do business."

Teach Clients to Help
Themselves and Each Other

Hairstylist Courtney Foster owns Courtney Foster Beauty in New York. Like other hands-on businesses, she was forced to close for much of 2020. Courtney responded by doubling down on social media.

First, she sent out social media posts and email blasts letting clients know that she was there for them if they needed any help. "Some of my clients don't even own a comb," Courtney says. "They let a professional do their hair." These people might need some help knowing what

Courtney Foster

Courtney Foster owns Courtney Foster Beauty in New York, NY. A conversation with Ted Gibson, who cut Angelina Jolie's hair, helped educate her about what makes a good haircut and inspired her to go to cosmetology school.

products to buy and how to use their purchases.

Then Courtney made demonstration videos that clients could download. "I used my son as a model," she said. "He got tired of me trying to wash his hair."

It was a natural progression when Courtney started coaching her clients and their loved ones on services they could perform for each other. Boyfriends cut hair over Zoom; husbands did relaxers, with Courtney guiding them every step of the way. "I could still be of service, doing what I love, by doing virtual consultations," she says. "It's not the full service that someone would get in the salon, but it helped with what I already had to help clients and keep myself busy." Clients were grateful, often paying more than she charged.

Courtney also paired with Swivel, a concierge system that helps African American women find people who specialize in working with African American hair. She did virtual consultations for these clients as well, and many of the New York–based customers are now clients at her reopened salon.

Not every client can safely come to the salon, so Courtney has continued with virtual services for those who want them. "One client is too scared to get on the train or drive to the salon from Brooklyn. I walked her boyfriend through doing a haircut, and he was phenomenal. Another client lives with her father, who has cancer. I did a virtual service for her as well. I put it on the schedule like any other service," Courtney says.

Find the Customers Who Value What You Offer

Letitia Hanke didn't close up shop after she dried her tears. She knew she couldn't force someone to hire a woman of color—and she didn't really want to work with customers who judged her, anyway. She could, however, find customers who saw her value, people who saw who she was as a plus.

Sometimes, the issue is too big to fix with a tweak to your business. You have to reframe it. You have to own it.

After that difficult day, Letitia went back to her office and shredded the couple's unsigned contract. She'd never call them again.

Then she set about rebranding the company, proudly displaying her first name—Letitia—and her face on everything: her advertisements, her website, everything.

Potential customers would know exactly who she is.

As it turns out, Northern California is home to many people who want to work with a Black-owned, woman-owned business. Letitia is thriving. Her business is a multimillion-dollar success story, with more growth on the way.

Letitia doesn't spend time with her former challengers. If she did, though, she would have a message for them. "I would thank those bullies now," she says. "They made me stronger. I have spent my whole life proving them wrong."

Questions to Consider

- If you're encountering a roadblock, is this a moment to double down or to think anew?

- What do you observe in your business? What's the data telling you?

- How can you be more flexible? Is there a way you can streamline your approach? Is there a new customer base to reach?

- Is there something that just isn't working for you that you might consider letting go?

- Is there anyone in your industry—an expert or even someone in your social network—you can talk to about the challenge you're facing?

SELF-MADE BOSSES

Leilani Baugh

Bobby Crocker

Sarah Korpela

Andrew Hypes

Min Park

Lisa O'Kelly

Keith Miller

Russ Kohler

Erin Caudell

Genevieve Weeks

CHAPTER 9

Growth and Scale

Leilani Baugh has never been accused of thinking too small.

A product of Oakland, California, Leilani is a chef who is always cooking up new ideas. She learned Chinese cooking from one of her grandmothers and Southern cooking from the other. Back in 2011, she started selling dishes from both traditions to customers from her home. Two years later, she catered a birthday brunch for a former police commissioner in San Francisco. After that, demand grew and she set her eyes on forming a full-fledged catering company.

That wasn't enough for Leilani. Six years later, she opened up two restaurants, Roux and Vine and the Magnolia Street Wine Lounge & Kitchen; she held residencies at Northern California wineries; and she put on pop-up events throughout the Bay Area. Now she's writing a cookbook.

"I've recognized that this could be really big," Leilani says. "I want restaurants, catering, and a cooking show. I also

Leilani Baugh

Leilani Baugh owns
Roux and Vine,
a restaurant in
Oakland, CA. She
grew up with a love
of food, learning
Southern cooking
from her Black
grandmother and
Chinese cooking
from her Chinese
grandmother.

plan to do an incubator kitchen for women of color, where they can learn the business and culinary sides and leave with their own businesses. That's the finish line."

It's an inspiring trajectory, and most business owners hope to achieve something like it one day themselves. But expanding your business doesn't happen on its own. You've got to navigate questions of strategy, timing, and capacity. In this chapter, we'll walk you through paths that can help you grow your business—on your terms.

◆ ◆ ◆

Growing your business can be intellectually engaging, challenging, and fun. Do it successfully and it will probably be good for your bank account—and your mental health.

You might even create jobs for other people and make a bigger impact on your community as a whole. There are a host of benefits to growing your business. But before we get into the steps you'll want to take to do just that, we want to be clear: Growing your business is a choice. You don't *have* to do it.

It's Okay to Stay Small

There is absolutely nothing wrong with running a business that stays about the same size, year after year. If it helps you pay your mortgage and gives you the flexibility you want in how you spend your time, it might be the perfect fit for your life. If it's working for you, keep doing it. There's no reason to change.

Here are a few reasons why you might decide to keep your business as-is.

You want to keep doing your current work. A goldsmith spends her days casting metal and setting gems. If she expands her shop by hiring more goldsmiths, she will inevitably trade some of the time she currently spends making jewelry for time spent supervising other makers. Doing what you love is more than enough reason to maintain the status quo.

You're the only one who can do your work. An artist can hire people to market her work, prep her canvases, and talk to collectors. But she probably can't pay another person to paint portraits for her.

You don't want the problems that come with a bigger business. Even a successful bigger business can bring additional responsibilities. You may carry those responsibilities around with you even after you've left the office. "More money, more problems," says Bobby Crocker, who owns LVLUP Fitness, a personalized training service. "If I opened up a string of training facilities, I would have

Bobby Crocker
Bobby Crocker owns LVLUP Fitness, a personalized training service in California's Bay Area. He is an ex-professional baseball player.

huge amounts of stress. I work to live. I don't live to work, though when I'm working, I'm all in."

Your business model thrives on exclusivity. Sarah Korpela, who owns Luxury Estate Managers of Aspen in Colorado, says that her business thrives on scarcity. She'll always keep her total number of properties at or below 35 houses. "I need to keep service to a very high standard, and that means staying small and specialized," she says. "I want the company brand to remain boutique and high end, and that means bigger isn't always better. It may not benefit my brand to grow if service and my standard is compromised."

Sarah Korpela
Sarah Korpela owns Luxury Estate Managers of Aspen in Aspen, CO. Her clients, she says, are able to treat their homes like five-star hotels: one call gets them whatever they need.

You want work-life balance. If you have caregiving responsibilities for your loved ones, or you simply prize the time you're able to travel or spend with your friends and family far more than working, you might not want to put in the early mornings and late nights it takes to expand your business beyond its current state. As Bobby Crocker noted, there are people who live to work and people who work to live. If you're the latter, and all of your needs are already met, consider keeping your business the same size it's always been.

How to Grow Business Revenue

SPECIALIST

Joey Rault
Joey Rault is the head of sales at Orum, a fintech company building the technology for real-time payments. Joey's work focuses on creating a better, more transparent and efficient financial infrastructure for businesses to thrive. Joey lives in NYC with his wife, Courtney.

Virtually every business owner, however, would be happy to make more money.

"The number one thing every business owner wants to talk about is revenue and how to grow it," says Joey Rault, a sales executive specializing in small businesses. "Business growth anchors on that revenue question."

Small businesses can grow revenue through a variety of strategies, from raising prices to expanding licensing. The rest of this chapter explores ways to grow revenue and scale your business.

Test Pricing Up and Down

Boosting prices could plump your bottom line without adding to your workload. Joey suggests that you look at your numbers to determine your best products—and then consider how much, when, and to whom you're selling them.

It might sound counterintuitive, but cutting prices can sometimes be the first step toward raising prices. "See how much more you sell if you offer a discount," he says.

If you sell more when you offer a discount, it might make sense to keep the price lower. However, if you sell the same amount as usual, it stands to reason that you're not going to suddenly bring in new customers because of the lower price tag. The best way for you to increase revenue may very well be by goosing your prices a bit.

Of course, you should test that hypothesis, too. If your sales numbers remain the same after you raise prices, keep the higher price. If they drop, you might want to lower them back to where you started. These types of tests help you understand the boundaries of this important lever—pricing.

It can always help to talk directly to your top customers about price. What would they like more of? How do your prices compare with your competitors? Is there a better structure for pricing that you hadn't thought of? There is a lot to learn by listening to the feedback of those who buy your product or service.

Knock on All the Doors

Andrew Hypes
Andrew Hypes is a DJ and producer based in Richmond, VA. He began playing the drums in the third grade.

Sometimes you have to push yourself out of your comfort zone.

Andrew Hypes used the same technique to get more gigs for his DJ business. "I found out who was in charge of hiring at clubs and bars, got in touch, explained who I am, and said, 'You should hire me,'" says the Waynesboro, Virginia, native. This can be uncomfortable to do, particularly at the beginning, but you get used to putting yourself out there. If you don't advocate for yourself, who will do it for you?

Expand by Brick and by Click

Moving your business to a new location or starting a second shop across town are obvious ways to expand your potential circle of customers. If you can afford to move to where there's more foot traffic, you'll probably see more customers. If your restaurant can fit a few more tables, you'll seat more customers and run more tabs. Min Park, a restaurant group consultant and investor, likes having restaurants with multiple locations, in part for this very reason.

Min Park
Min Park is an ex-finance professional (JPMorgan) who invests in hospitality concepts such as Rooster & Rice and Itria, technology, real estate, and cryptocurrency.

Expanding your presence doesn't always mean making your physical space bigger—you can explore online sales, too.

"Two kinds of businesses sell online," says Weebly founder David Rusenko. "Startups often choose to sell online before they sell in person, and established businesses also move from 'brick' to also having a 'click' presence. Maybe they've already done some Instagram and Etsy, and that leads naturally to setting up their own online order pages."

Selling online can sometimes lead to exponential expansion. Build a hit product and sell it in a store, a craft fair, or

SPECIALIST

David Rusenko
David Rusenko is the general manager of e-commerce at Square in San Francisco, CA. He was the founder and CEO of Weebly.

farmers' market, and your customer pool is limited to the people who happen to attend the market or walk in the door when you're open. The internet never closes. Selling online means that you don't have to make every sale face-to-face, and you don't have to set business hours, either. If an order comes in at night while you're asleep, you can just ship it the next morning.

"Buyers are increasingly shopping wherever and whenever is convenient for them," David says. "The pandemic only intensified that trend."

Avoid the Common Pitfalls of Selling Online

In considering online sales, many business owners think only of managing the transaction: accepting a credit card online and processing that payment. But selling online can be a lot more complicated. To do it well, you really should use a technological platform that helps you coordinate your operation.

This is particularly important if you're selling both in person and online. Any shoe store, for example, has a limited number of shoes. You don't want a situation in which a customer buys a size 9 pair of heels in the store when someone just clicked "buy" on that same pair online—especially if you don't have a product inventory that includes more than one pair of that size 9.

The more ways you sell, the more complicated the problem can become, a challenge restaurants often confront.

That's because many dining establishments don't just sell to in-house diners. They also deliver to people calling in on the phone, through their own website, and through food-delivery services like Grubhub, DoorDash, Instacart, or Postmates. That can lead to a backup in the kitchen if you're not prepared to handle the rush.

Here's how you can streamline these problems. The first, and most important, step is making sure you're set up correctly on the technological front. That doesn't mean you have to hire a new IT manager. Toast, Clover, PayPal, Square, and Shopify make platforms that can help you manage inventory that you're selling through multiple avenues. These services offer ready-made systems that are easy to learn and effective at solving problems. They combine a digital point of sale with the ability to accept payments both online and offline. In the context of restaurants, Toast and Square, for example, offer an explicit workflow that helps manage the kitchen and keep track of orders coming in from online, delivery, and in-person diners. There are many options for systems, and it's worth exploring whether there is one that's specific to your industry. Shopify provides a platform for online sales and has broad functionality for getting up and running quickly with a professional ecommerce business. Look at the features and test it out.

Streamlining your sales channels is another strategic way to handle this problem, David says. This means you try to funnel the number of places people buy your product to as small a number as possible. For example, if you acquire customers on Etsy, shift them to a direct relationship via your company website as quickly as possible rather than continuing to sell to them through Etsy. This could mean following up with an email or including a coupon for exclusive products bought through your website when you deliver the initial purchase.

That said, be careful not to build too many platforms that are disconnected and hard to maintain. Think through a customer's logic with simple examples of how you would buy things. As you re-create the customer journey, you will see the potential problems that arise with how you plan to build out the technology to support your business—and you will be able to identify solutions, too.

Build Relationships with Larger Retailers

Lisa O'Kelly
Lisa O'Kelly is cofounder of Zellee Organic, based in Maui, HI. The company makes an organic, plant-based fruit jel snack that uses konjac, a plant from East Asia, to gel the product, instead of gelatin.

Another option is to get someone else to sell your products, too.

Hawaii-based Zellee started out selling its fruit-based jel snack online and at local grocery stores in Hawaii and California, where the company's two founders live. Zellee co-owner Lisa O'Kelly said they were looking for more options to boost sales, so they started talking to natural food distributors.

To get a distributor, companies typically need to prove that there is already consumer demand for their product. In

Zellee's case, that meant collecting letters from local grocery stores that already carried their product and hiring a brokerage firm to send representatives to persuade new stores to stock Zellee.

Zellee also hired a consulting firm to get in front of bigger grocery stores, such as Whole Foods, Safeway, or Kroger, which have set category review schedules. The consulting firm explained how the system worked, then helped them pitch Whole Foods in Southern California at the appropriate time. Hiring the consultant was a little like hiring an agent, O'Kelly says. The consultant has relationships with decision makers at these larger stores, and clients benefit from those connections.

These new distribution relationships, made possible through hard work and investing in outside help, have allowed Zellee to boost sales. It's an investment that's paid off in partnerships with more than 100 new stores selling Zellee's product.

The company's next step is big-box stores, such as Target and Walmart. "Most large retailers would like you to buy advertising in their circulars and online platforms, as well as donate to their foundations. Some have slotting fees where you pay to be on the shelf, like renting shelf space," Lisa says. Again, an investment like this could very well pay off, as long as you're sure that once your product is available to customers, they will buy it.

Zellee currently runs distribution from a warehouse in Fresno, California, and also fulfills website orders out of Lisa's garage. "We send out 15 to 20 packages a day, plus samples to retailers and influencers," she says. Fulfillment will need to change when the company starts distributing with Target and Walmart, as volume will increase substantially, but that's a problem that Lisa and cofounder Eriko Dowd are happy to have.

Sell Adjacent Products or Services

If you're looking to grow, you might also think about expanding into new product lines. What other items and services do your customers already buy? Are you interested in providing anything on that list?

Keith Miller
Keith and Patrycia Miller own Bubbly Paws Dog Wash in Minneapolis, MN. Keith sometimes brings his employees cupcakes.

In St. Paul, Minnesota, Bubbly Paws owner Keith Miller got into the dog-grooming business because he was already running a dog daycare. "People kept asking if their dogs could get clean at the daycare," Keith says. "Our daycare space wasn't big enough to add grooming, so we opened Bubbly Paws as a second business."

This kind of expansion in verticals is an even better plan if you use it to distinguish your business from the competition. Heber Valley Milk & Artisan Cheese, located in Midway, Utah, was just a dairy farm before owner Russ Kohler adjusted its model. "We needed to do something different, and we hit on artisanal cheese," he says. Unlike competitors who simply process and sell milk, Heber Valley makes and sells cheddar, Monterey jack, queso fresco, and a Finnish-style cheese called juustoleipä. Now the business is selling something unique, rather than just something that's often considered a commodity. "It is hard to quantify how much my business actually grew, because it morphed into an entirely different business model, but I would say my revenue has gone up about 800 percent over what it was 10 years ago when we started," Russ says.

Russ Kohler
Russ Kohler is in the fourth generation of his family to run Heber Valley Milk & Artisan Cheese in Midway, UT. Adding artisanal cheese helped Heber Valley to stand out among area dairies.

Find a Partner

It might not be a forever solution, but if you want to dip your toes into a larger market, a partnership or trade might let you try on the experience and see if you like it. A partnership can add working capital, provide fresh ideas, bring new skills, offer a valuable trade, or just divide the labor of starting and running a small business.

When the growth of her business was just beginning to accelerate, Leilani Baugh began catering out of a space in a busy commercial kitchen. That gave her more room than she'd had in her kitchen, where she'd started out. But in order to use that space, she had to pay rent.

Leilani took the offer because it gave her access to a much less expensive kitchen from which she could fulfill her catering orders and let her provide customers with somewhere to sit and eat during her pop-ups. The arrangement lasted a year and couldn't have been more successful. It gave Leilani a steady income as she was growing her business. "It also gave me an opportunity to see if owning a restaurant was really what I wanted to do," she says.

Focus on Repeat Sales

Given a choice between a new customer and a repeat customer, you want a repeat every time. Why?

- Getting a new customer can cost five times more than retaining an existing customer. New customers need to discover who you are, where you are, and what you can do for them—all things you might have to spend marketing dollars to accomplish. Existing customers have all that information already.
- Existing customers are also between 3 and 12 times more likely to buy from you than new customers. They know your work and they're already fans, so they don't have the hesitations about whether they'll be happy with a purchase that a new client might have.

Bobby Crocker is a good example of a business owner who has benefited from the power of repeat business. When injury ended his career as a professional baseball player, he decided to use his skills to train others. "I put an ad in the local paper and started getting clients right away," he says. But there was a problem. Personalized training isn't a product that enables consistency in scheduling.

So Bobby made a change. Rather than selling an hourly product, he switched to selling camps, video training, and team training. Now, he works with a variety of schools on youth fitness in addition to his one-on-one sessions—and his schedule is much more predictable.

Here's the key: With this new model, most of his clients come back to him again and again, both for individual time and for their broader families. He's lost the effort and expense of finding new customers—an especially draining process when every customer is a new customer—and gained a business in which most of his hours and time are driven by school and camp sign-ups.

Sell Other People's Products

Erin Caudell
Erin Caudell and her partner, Franklin Pleasant, co-own The Local Grocer in Flint, MI. They are longtime food activists and newer farmers, working to make sure every community has access to nutrient-dense foods.

Erin Caudell co-owns The Local Grocer, a farm-to-shelf, community-based agriculture and specialty store in Flint, Michigan. Three days a week, she also sells her farm's goods at a stand at Flint's downtown farmer's market. At both outlets, The Local Grocer supplements the food from its own farm with food produced by other people. "At the farmer's market, we get elk and venison through a supplier, milk from an Amish dairy in northern Michigan, and fruit and locally produced pantry products from other suppliers," Erin says.

Erin adds that her store has bought produce from perhaps 25 different farmers, which she says is especially useful for niche products like mushrooms. It's sometimes difficult, though, to find vendors who will provide produce that doesn't need a lot of washing or trimming. "It needs to be consistently nice, not hit and miss," she says. "That's a lot more labor, either time spent in technical assistance or at the sink, and it's sometimes not worth the time."

That's the key when you're selling goods from other suppliers; you've got to price it right. Make sure to include the wholesale cost to you, as well as any labor and time costs, in the final price tag the customer sees. Only then can you be sure you're making a sustainable profit.

Use a Subscription Model

The Local Grocer also sells community-supported agriculture, or CSA, shares for its farm. CSA shares are essentially a subscription plan in which consumers pay a single price for weekly shares of produce throughout the growing season. If a farm has a bumper crop, customers get the benefit of that. If conditions aren't as good, their weekly shares are smaller.

"We built it up to about 40 families as CSA members, and then we teamed up with two other farms to make a CSA that sells food for 26 weeks a year to 125 members," Erin says. Customers benefit because they know that they'll get fresh food every week. The Local Grocer and its partner farms benefit because they're able to presell their produce, often before putting seeds in the ground, giving much more certainty to their farming operations.

Subscription models can also work in a variety of other industries. Let's say you make skincare products. You might invite customers to set up a subscription in which they get a new jar of hand cream every three months, while also giving them the option of buying one jar at a time. A restaurant could offer customers a flat monthly price for one delivered meal every week. These models allow for more stability in your month-to-month income—and allow you a greater ability to plan ahead for this more consistent demand.

License or Franchise Your Business Model

You can even grow your business by letting other people run it. This could take the form of licensing, where someone else pays you for permission to manufacture a product based on your intellectual property; or franchising, where another person pays you a fee plus ongoing royalties in return for use of your trademark, ongoing support, and the right to use your system of doing business while selling your product or service.

San Francisco's Tutu School is an example of a successful franchise operation.

With multiple, constant stressors on their bodies, most ballet dancers have short careers. Genevieve Weeks knew that firsthand when she moved to San Francisco to dance with the Oakland Ballet—so it wasn't long before she started thinking about what she would do when she retired from performing.

Genevieve Weeks
A retired professional ballet dancer, Genevieve Weeks owns Tutu School, a franchised operation that offers ballet classes for toddlers and kids. She is based in Chicago, IL, and San Francisco, CA.

Tutu School, a ballet school for children, was the answer. It was the perfect way for Genevieve to continue her passion, and her paycheck.

"I opened the first school in San Francisco in 2008," Genevieve says. "It was me and a tiny room on the edge of the North Beach neighborhood. There started to be an explosion in children's services, coinciding with a baby boom of children entering toddlerhood in San Francisco. No one in the dance space had caught up with that."

This all happened in the middle of one of the steepest economic downturns the country had ever seen. Even in a recession, Genevieve found, people still spend money on their children. With some luck and a whole lot of hard work, Tutu School was an immediate hit.

Genevieve soon hired another teacher. Then she started another Tutu School in Marin, where some of her kindergarten-age students had moved. A year later, Genevieve realized that Tutu School could thrive anywhere there are children. That's when she began to think about franchising the business.

A friend, who had recently franchised her wedding apparel business, referred Genevieve to her franchise attorney. "It was intimidating when we first met with her to find out everything involved in franchising," Genevieve says. The list included trademarking the logo, incorporating as an LLC for the two Bay Area locations, and establishing an S corporation for the franchising operation. (You can find more about legal structures for small businesses in Chapter 3, "Legal Matters.")

Perhaps most important, she began systematizing everything about the business. Instead of registering dancers with a series of spreadsheets, she moved to using studio management software created specifically for the business. She created a more robust curriculum and training materials, instead of simply training teachers by having them follow her.

"Even if you have no intention of scaling through franchising, it's useful to go through the exercise of considering how you'd run your own business," Genevieve says. "There's no downside to systematizing your business, really looking at your systems and operations."

Do that earlier rather than later, she says. It will give you a sense of whether a business can be replicated. Plus, your existing business will run more smoothly.

Weeks's little dance business has blossomed into 37 Tutu School locations, 34 of them franchises. Eight more are sold but not yet open, and 10 are reserved. The franchising relationship works well for both Genevieve and the independent operators. Franchisees pay both a purchase price and a royalty on gross sales.

Most franchisees operate multiple locations. Some of them, like Genevieve, are making a retirement plan for their post-dance lives. Others are past Tutu School parents who have corporate backgrounds and want a family-friendly, flexible business.

But while franchising her business has worked out well for the most part, Genevieve says there are also drawbacks. "I expected more passive income than I'm finding," she says. "It's a decent amount of work to support franchises."

There's a big difference between licensing a concept, which is more hands-off, and franchising, which is a true partnership. For example, on top of Genevieve's hands-on support for franchisees, Tutu School uses an internal platform called Twirl to provide online training, documents, and a library of marketing pieces, such as print advertising and postcards. But for her, these steps are worth it.

"I was worried about being consistent across the brand, especially when we just had a few locations," Genevieve says. With more locations, she feels that the company has actually given her business stronger communications around brand standards and provides better training and resources than it would if it were just the original school.

Plus, broader ownership means that more people have a stake in the business, and their suggestions come from wanting nothing but success for the company. Since she began franchising, ideas from franchisees have improved the business in countless ways—because what works in one market usually is worth adding across the board.

"No one has to reinvent the wheel, and the wheel keeps getting better," Genevieve says.

Use Free Resources

As you're looking to expand your business, take advantage of the wide variety of resources offering free advice.

Heber Valley, the milk and artisanal cheese seller, worked with Goldman Sachs's free 10,000 Small Businesses program, which helped them create farm visit experiences that show off their products and processes. Owner Russ Kohler also spent time with an MBA class from a local university, which suggested different packaging. "They said that we should get away from a commodity look, so we stopped cutting our cheese in a block and changed the packaging," Russ says.

When he worked with Utah's Own, a Utah program that promotes in-state products, Russ also found a marketer and website developer—even though those services weren't officially offered by the state.

And as we said in Chapter 1, don't forget about the Small Business Administration! The SBA is set up to help you, from finding funding to connecting you with a business coach.

The honest truth is that starting a business is hard and expanding one can be even harder, which is why this work isn't for everyone. But if you do want to grow your revenue, boost your sales, or expand your geographic footprint, there are plenty of options—and resources—available to help you do it.

Questions to Consider

- Who are some partners and resources in your industry or adjacent industries that might help you grow your business? Have you tapped them for advice?

- What other businesses might sell your products or services? What other products might you be willing to sell?

- Could you grow your business by finding a new audience online?

- Does your business lend itself to multiple locations or distribution outside your immediate geographical reach? How much of your business can you systematize?

- Would it make sense to expand your business through licensing or franchising? How replicable is what you're doing?

CHAPTER 10

Transitions

Harry Taub had been a dentist for more than four decades when he decided he was ready for a change.

He didn't feel like he could just close the doors of his practice and walk away. He had valuable equipment for his practice and patients he cared about too much to leave behind. He also had no one in his life ready to take over. His team was too junior and his kids had no professional experience with—or interest in—teeth.

Thankfully, Harry had another option. A private equity firm, which already owned 250 dental practices, offered the highest price for Harry's Flourtown, Pennsylvania, practice in a bidding war. Part of the deal, however, was that Harry would continue with the business to see it through to a stable transition.

This left Harry, who still owns a piece of the practice, with more free time and less control of his business, a trade-off

Harry Taub
Harry Taub is a partially retired dentist in Flourtown, PA. He's also a bassoonist and an avid golfer.

many entrepreneurs confront after they sell their companies. For Harry, it's been challenging to let go.

"It's been harder than I imagined to have a backseat view to changes in the organization," he said.

If he had it to do over again, Harry says that he would have arranged for a quicker transition out of the business so that he didn't have to see it transform. "I kind of knew what I was getting into," he explained, "but I didn't know what it would feel like."

Harry isn't alone. For so many entrepreneurs, the hardest part of building a company is knowing when it's time to leave it. No matter how ready you are to move on, it's hard to say good-bye to a business you've put your blood, sweat, tears—and money—into building.

More often than not, there will come a day when it's time to enter the next chapter of your life, whether that's retirement or another passion or professional opportunity. When that time does arrive, you'll want to be ready.

That's why, for small business owners, as important as it is to think about how to start your business, it's just as important to think about how you might one day transition away from it.

Building a Business Someone Else Could Run

We'll level with you: Building any business is hard. Building one you can leave behind is even harder.

According to the Exit Planning Institute, 80 percent of companies with annual revenues of less than $50 million never sell—and just 30 percent of family businesses survive into the second generation. Meanwhile, many owners that do sell end up unhappy that they did.

When people can't sell or otherwise transition their business to someone else, or when they are disappointed with the terms of the sale, it's often because they haven't created a business that's ready to be sold.

Before you start thinking about transitioning out, you've got to be very honest with yourself. Look at your financial profile and consider whether another person could successfully run your firm. Is your business profitable? Are you well positioned in your market? Is the business growing and building market share? Is it durable? Can it scale up over time? If the answer to any of these questions is no, you'll want to take the time to plan for and execute moves that will make your business more attractive to potential buyers.

Generally, the best acquisition targets share three—ideally, four—qualities. First, they're profitable. Second, their assets are desirable. Third, their prospects for the future are strong. And fourth, they have something unique to offer. It might be a creative solution to a common problem, like technology or intellectual property. Or it might be something as simple as unique customer lists, an advantageous location, or other assets, like customized equipment.

Michael A. Sutherland Brown is CEO of Teamshares, a Brooklyn company that helps employees buy their companies

SPECIALIST

**Michael A.
Sutherland Brown**
Michael A.
Sutherland Brown is
CEO of Teamshares,
a Brooklyn, NY,
company that helps
employees buy their
companies when
an owner retires.
He sees digital
businesses and those
that combine physical
and digital presences
as very attractive
to buyers. "Digital
businesses can
have as high as a 90
percent success rate
in selling, whereas
old economy
businesses can be
as low as 20 to 30
percent," he says.

when an owner retires. He sees digital businesses and those that combine physical and digital presences as very attractive to buyers. "Ninety percent of digital businesses are ones that owners can sell," he says.

If that describes your business, make sure the world knows it, even if you're not planning to sell the company anytime soon. Start networking. Let competitors and adjacent businesses know what you're doing. One day, they may come to you with an intriguing offer.

Your networking should extend beyond the people and companies you think are logical buyers for your firm—especially when the logical buyers are in the same field. After all, a competitor might prefer continued competition to paying top dollar for your business, while someone who isn't yet in your field might put a higher premium on the assets you've built.

Keeping Your Business in the Family

Many small business owners hope that their children will inherit and run their businesses, but as Brown puts it, "That option either exists or it doesn't."

"Sometimes families do run a business for three generations or more, but it's very rare," he explained. "The hardest things I've seen with children inheriting businesses are two difficult interpersonal dynamics: First, the founder has to let go. Second, the next generation has to want the business."

These are difficult challenges, but sometimes passing a business down from generation to generation works out—as has been the case for Brooklyn, New York–based Acme Smoked Fish.

Acme Smoked Fish started in 1906 with Harry Brownstein, who delivered smoked fish door-to-door as a jobber on the Lower East Side of Manhattan. He bought smoked fish from several small smokehouses and delivered it to his customers. In 1954, he and his son-in-law opened their own smoked fish plant and decided to name it Acme—not only because that word means "the best" but also because they knew it would be one of the first businesses listed in the Yellow Pages. (In the era when Yellow Pages were relevant, that's the kind of creative, smart thinking that helped a small business transform into a big one!)

Eventually, Harry's great-grandchildren inherited the company. Four generations later, several of them still run it. They saw new possibilities for the firm, taking it from a small, family-run business to a global enterprise, says Emily Caslow Gindi, a co-owner and Acme's customer service manager.

This growth, Emily says, can be traced in part to the fact that they had the foresight to upgrade their manufacturing capabilities. At the time, the investment felt like a risk, but it's since turned out to be critical to the company's ability to scale while prioritizing health and safety.

The current generation has had to navigate issues of equality—they own the company in equal shares—and fair compensation for each person's role. Emily took time away from the business to raise young children while her brother and cousin kept working there. When she came back, they all decided it made the most sense for her brother and cousin to keep running the business. They recognized that an older sister reporting to her younger brother might get complicated, so they reworked their management structures, because as Emily says, "we're committed to having our own adult relationships."

Emily Caslow Gindi
Emily Caslow Gindi is a fourth-generation family member and owner of Acme Smoked Fish Corporation. Acme manufactures and distributes smoked seafood throughout the United States and worldwide.

That commitment has been vital to running a successful business with people who also spend Thanksgiving together. "The reason we've made it this far is that we're family first," Emily says. "We can be really mad at each other and totally disagree at work, but we treat each other well."

That said, even with the best intentions—and working relationships—transitions within family-run businesses will always remain complex. No matter how you spin it, day-to-day interactions can be complicated when two people are both coworkers and relatives.

Keeping a business in the family can also make estate planning tricky, says Judith McGee, a financial planner in Portland, Oregon. It's often difficult for business-owning parents to leave family members equal shares of an estate when only some of the heirs actually operate the business.

"It's not always possible to make the inheritance fair," McGee says, adding that she sees this with farmers and ranchers. "There might be a son who has worked with Dad and has his confidence. The daughters got married and another son went off and did something else. In many cases, the first son gets the lion's share—and if he helped build the business, he thinks that he deserves to have what he created."

Judith McGee
Judith McGee is CEO, cofounder, and wealth manager at McGee Wealth Management in Portland, OR. Many of her clients own small businesses.

Likewise, sales within a family can be difficult. Even if one or more children do want a company, they might find it difficult to pay what it's worth. McGee herself is considering selling her financial-planning firm to a larger company, in part because her daughter and another minority shareholder don't have the funds to buy her out. "They'd have to raise a significant amount of money," she says.

Transitioning Ownership to Your Employees

Your employees could buy your company, either individually or as a group. This option can work well, but you'll need a few pieces to fall into place. First, you, the owner, need to be willing to step down. Second, you'll need one or more of your employees to be excited about running your business—and able to do it. And third, you'll have to arrive at a price all parties can feel good about.

Brown, who deals with these transactions often at Teamshares, has seen that selling a small business to an individual is the most common arrangement. "The buyer is usually someone in her forties or fifties who doesn't have a lot of expertise in buying or selling businesses. She might be getting an SBA loan and is probably offering 90 percent cash up front, which de-risks the transaction for the seller," Brown says.

You could also sell your company to its employees through an employee stock ownership plan, or ESOP. To support an ESOP, a business needs at least 20 employees, and it needs to be successful enough to carry some debt, as it will either pay out the owner over a period of time, need to take out a bank loan, or rely on a combination of the two.

If you sell your company to an ESOP and the ESOP chooses to become an S corporation, the company's income passes through to the ESOP—and since ESOPs are exempt, it won't need to pay any taxes.

Without the burden of having to write a check to the government, the ESOP will have that much more money available to buy out the owner—otherwise known as you. There are many more pros and cons associated with selling to an ESOP, so it's worth the time to research if the structure is right for your business.

Selling to Another Company

It's also possible that another firm will want to buy your company. In many cases, it won't come knocking on your door. You've got to do your own research. Brown recommends finding at least 50 companies that might want to buy yours. "You could work with an attorney to do this," he said. "You could also do it yourself, if you have the time."

Even if you do that research yourself, talking with an investment banker or attorney who specializes in advising small business owners about selling can be helpful early in the sales process. That's especially true if you're not familiar with how selling works.

A few tried-and-true tips can help you as you're preparing for a sale.

Decide When You'll Sell

Business owners typically sell when their personal timing, financial planning, and estate planning converge.

Like Harry, who sold his dentistry practice to another firm, many owners sell when they're ready to retire. Others sell because their health makes it difficult to continue working as they age. Maybe their health is fine, but running the business is too stressful, or the business has grown past their ability to manage it, sometimes because market trends are moving away from an owner's skill set.

Regardless of your motivation, you'll want to plan a sale for a good time in the broader economy. Even if your company is performing well, you may find selling difficult if interest rates, your industry, or the overall economy aren't trending to your advantage. Be mindful of these exogenous factors so that you don't get stuck selling at the least opportune time.

Don't Wait Too Long

You might imagine that you want to keep running the company for as long as its prospects are bright—but that sunny projection is exactly what will attract buyers and persuade them to pay a healthy price for your business.

Likewise, if you're planning for a sale in a few years, but a seller materializes before your planned timeline, be willing to be flexible. A deal may not be there for you at exactly the moment you're looking for it.

Run the Company

When you're thinking seriously about selling your company, it can be tempting to mentally move along to your next step. Resist that temptation. You need to present potential buyers with a business that's running at full strength. If you're too busy with the sale, you can enlist a key employee to run the company for you, but either way, make sure it's not slowing down precisely when you are trying to sell it.

Even if you're planning to transition out, for as long as you're at your company, run it as though you are going to stay there for the long term. There will be a temptation to skimp on what you invest into the business, as you ask yourself whether the purchase price will refund your investment. But if you cut corners, that will be reflected in the size of the offers you receive for your company. Additionally, a purchaser may want you to stay in place for two to five years after the sale to ensure a smooth transition.

Clean House

Selling is a complex process, and you want your business to be ready. Before you talk to potential buyers, clearly document your company. This is the time to create or update your capital structure, financial reports, and other records. Hiring an accountant—who might or might not be your regular accountant—to create orderly documentation will help potential buyers understand your business. Even if a business that's under a drift of paperwork is actually in good shape, no one wants to buy a mess.

"You need at least three and ideally five years of clean, clear, professionally organized records," Brown says. "QuickBooks is fine. Make sure you understand and can talk about the financials. Understand the cost of goods sold. Give accurate expenses and profit margins. People often imagine that they earn more than they do."

If you've mixed your company with your hobbies or other parts of your personal life, disentangle them. Stop raiding the petty cash box when your wallet is empty. If your business is paying for personal expenses—anything from a car to magazine subscriptions—change the way that you're funding these. If you're running a sideline that's part business and part hobby from the same books that you use for your main business, separate the two. Replace fuzzy boundaries with crisp lines around your primary business.

You cannot sell a business in which you perform every function, because without you, everything will collapse. If you haven't already, begin building a team and processes that would help someone else run the company. Document the things you do.

Try to get long-term contracts or noncompete agreements with your key employees. Document any verbal understandings you have with shareholders and employees, especially with anyone who has invested money in the business or received ownership shares.

As you're cleaning up shop, fix any problems that you find. It'll put you in a better position to sell and forestall potential issues with a buyer. Buyers don't care for surprises. There's a market for imperfect businesses; indeed, this is the only kind of business that exists. But no one wants to reach a deal, only to be surprised. Try to discuss all your information about the business, eliminating or limiting last-minute hiccups. That improves the odds that the deal will close.

Negotiate a Deal

Make a complete, organized presentation to potential buyers. Focus on earnings and opportunities for growth. If there are multiple possible bidders, give all of them the same information at the same time.

Meanwhile, decide what you most want from this sale. Maybe you want the highest price, or maybe you care a lot about the next owner doing right by your employees or keeping the business in the same geographical location.

There are an unlimited number of variables that factor into every negotiation, so make sure you're asking yourself questions from a variety of angles: Is this the right market for selling my business? Will key customers stay with the company if I sell? Do I have any potential deal-breakers in sale terms?

When the time comes to make your pitch, don't state an asking price. Put out too high a number, and you'll scare buyers away. Give a number that's too low, and you leave money on the table. Let prospective buyers tell you what they think the business is worth.

Companies typically sell based on industry-specific multiples as a standard way to compare operating performance. The most common metric is multiples of operating profit, or EBITDA (earnings before interest, taxes, depreciation, and amortization). Advisors, attorneys, or people who have sold other businesses can give you a sense of the multiples that are typical for your industry. In addition to financial multiples, there can be operating multiples that inform valuation too. Operational metrics include price/active customers, price/recurring revenue, and more industry-specific metrics. These multiples let you create a mental estimate that you can compare against the offers you receive.

Keep in mind that money up front is just one potential element of a deal. You might take less money from a buyer who agrees to other desirable terms—like a shorter transition out of your role at the company. As Harry Taub discovered with his dentistry practice, staying on at your company after the sale can give you a little more control over how your assets are treated, but it's not a perfect solution.

"If you're selling your business, you need to be prepared to leave your business," he says. "You might not agree with the new owner, and it will cause you a lot of agita to sit there and watch them change the business that was your lifeline. It's tough to go from being the boss to being an employee. It would have been easier for me to leave earlier."

A buyer also might want to pay you a percentage of the business's performance after the sale to ensure that you'll work hard to make the change of ownership a success. Called an earnout, this can be a bridge between the parties' different estimates of what a company is worth. An earnout might be based on a product clearing regulators' approval, for instance, or on the sales or profits from a particular product or piece of intellectual property. When this happens, the buyer is essentially asking you to hold the note while allowing them to pay you over time.

Alternatives to Selling Your Business

If you can't find an outside buyer, or if transitioning ownership to a family member or employee isn't working out, simply shutting down your business is a viable alternative to selling. It's less lucrative, obviously, but it's also much less complicated.

As a financial planner, Judith suggests that business owners avoid having all their wealth in their business. "Take some of that wealth out of your business during your working lifetime," she says. "Under-live your income, take distributions, and keep your debt down." When your eventual retirement and estate planning don't depend on selling your company, you have more options.

Another choice might give you flexibility now and set you up well for an eventual sale: Hire someone to run the company and stay on as the owner. The person you hire could be an external hire or internal promotion. Either way, that person's success depends on your willingness to move to a different role.

This strategy is rare, but it can be a good one, Brown says. It's also a step toward a future sale, in that it shows that the business can succeed without you. "It buys back your time and makes your company super salable, while also taking the pressure off if you decide not to sell right away," Brown says. "You might start another business, travel, or pursue a hobby."

We know that when you're starting a company, the last thing you want to do is think about how you're going to leave it. For many of you, this chapter might not be relevant for decades. But odds are, there will come a time when you want out. Whether you sell your business, hand it over to a loved one, or shut it down, you should do so proud of what you built and prepared for whatever life has in store next.

After all, when you reach that point, you'll have proven to everyone, most importantly yourself, that you're a self-made boss in every sense of the word. Once you can say that, there's not much you can't do.

Let's face it—sometimes things don't always go as planned and entrepreneurs have to make difficult decisions on whether or not it is time to wind down their business. If you have exhausted all potential financing resources and there is no potential buyer of your enterprise, it may be time to adopt a more "defensive strategy" in order to mitigate personal liability associated with winding down your business.

First and foremost, you need to come up with a realistic assessment of how much runway you have to maintain operations. Unanticipated costs that can equal several weeks of operations can pop up during the wind-down process. Importantly, there are some expenses, like paying compensation or sales taxes and fiduciary duties to creditors, which if not satisfied as a legal matter prior to the wind-down of the business could result in director or officer liability. Getting ahead of these unanticipated costs is important and requires careful review of the company's financial information with the advice of financial and legal counsel.

While the process can be daunting (and of course disappointing given the desired outcome), by partnering with counsel and other advisers you can take key steps to mitigate personal liability and make the wind-down process as smooth as possible.

Questions to Consider

- When is the right time for you to consider transitioning out of your business? Who would be a good fit to take over?

- Do you have advisors who can help you with significant corporate transactions? If not, do you know where to look for them?

- How important is it to you that your business thrives after you transition out of ownership? Are you willing to stay on for a period to preserve what you've built?

- Are there revenues or expenses that would change once you are no longer the owner?

Index

About the Authors

Photo by Annie Barnett

Jackie Reses is the chief executive officer of Luna Financial Group, a fintech building banking infrastructure for fintech and crypto companies. Previously, she was the executive chairman of Square Financial Services and capital lead and head of the People Team at Square (now Block Inc). Square Capital is one of the largest lenders to small businesses in the United States. Prior to Square, Jackie was the chief development officer for Yahoo! and the head of the US media group at Apax Partners, one of the largest global private equity firms. Jackie also spent seven years at Goldman Sachs in mergers and acquisitions and the principal investment area.

She has been named one of *Forbes*'s Self-Made Women, *Fast Company*'s Most Creative People in Business, and *American Banker*'s Most Powerful Woman in Finance. Jackie is also on the board of directors of Endeavor, Affirm, and Nubank and is the chairman of the Economic Advisory Council of the Federal Reserve Bank of San Francisco. Jackie received a bachelor's degree in economics with honors from the Wharton School of the University of Pennsylvania after growing up in Atlantic City, New Jersey. She has earned multiple patents for inventions in financial technology, payments, and cryptocurrency.

Photo by Jordan Rosner

Lauren Weinberg is the chief marketing and communications officer at Square, driving marketing and comms strategy globally, which includes investment decisions, optimization of marketing channels, brand strategy, analytics, marketing technology, creative execution, and communications. As part of her remit, she is responsible for managing Square's entire marketing budget to ensure the company achieves its revenue and brand goals. She also directs the channel and creative strategy across all of Square's marketing channels, including search, online display, organic social and content, email, television, audio, and digital video. Prior to Square, Lauren was the founder of LMW Consulting, a strategic advisory firm assisting startups and established businesses alike in marketing strategy. Before consulting, Lauren served as Yahoo!'s vice president of marketing strategy and insights, where she oversaw media planning and buying, brand and marketing effectiveness research, consumer analytics, and industry research. Prior to Yahoo!, Lauren was vice president of digital insights and research at Viacom. She spent the three previous years at Advertising.com as director of research and worked at Nielsen and comScore as a media analyst and product manager, respectively.

Lauren serves on the board of the Mobile Marketing Association and Emory University's Quantitative Theories and Methods department. She's also an advisor to several startups and an ongoing advisor of The Women's Startup Lab, a leading accelerator for female founders. She's an executive mentor as part of *AdWeek*'s executive mentorship program. Lauren is an experienced storyteller with a background in journalism who is often featured on podcasts and in trade publications. Lauren was named to the 2020 *Forbes* Next CMO list and as one of the Top 30 Most Influential Fintech Marketers in 2021. Lauren received her bachelor's degree from Emory University. She currently lives in New Jersey with her husband, two sons, and two dogs.